The Winter of My Repose

Linda McGovern

PublishAmerica
Baltimore

First printing

PublishAmerica has allowed this work to remain exactly as the author intended, verbatim, without editorial input.

ISBN: 978-1-61546-391-6
PUBLISHED BY PUBLISHAMERICA, LLLP
www.publishamerica.com
Baltimore

Printed in the United States of America

DEDICATION

For my loving husband, family and friends; who without their love and support I might not have made it through this life altering event. But most of all I would like to dedicate this book to all of the doctors who participated in the endeavor to save my life. If it wasn't for them, I would not be here today to tell this story.

PROLOGUE

No one wants to die. In fact, most people don't think about death on a daily basis. The majority of us would like to live to a ripe old age, enjoying all that living has to offer. But the truth of the matter is; we're all going to die. It's just a question of when and how. I can honestly admit I, like many others, never considered my demise, until it came knocking at my door.

My name is Linda. I am fifty-three years old, have been married for thirty years and have three sons. As I sit and gaze out of my window, I reflect upon three years ago, the winter of my repose. Scars from that time in my life are etched deep within my soul.

To be fully honest, I wish I could say I had been happy before I realized I might die, but I know I wasn't. My illness made me realize what was important in my life. When my brain tumor was discovered I was still recovering from the tremendous pain caused by my husband's affair with another woman. Although I considered leaving him, I consciously made the decision to remain with my family, hoping we could reconcile what had happened. I often wonder if I chose this path because of the need to keep our family together or if perhaps someone in a higher place led me to that decision. This is something that you, the reader, can decide.

THE BEGINNING

The August afternoon was sunny with wisps of clouds floating in the sky. My husband Neil and I owned The Inn, a restaurant and bar overlooking the lake. On days like this, people came from miles around to enjoy the view from our deck.

The Inn is located in a tiny village called Speculator in the Adirondack Mountains. We opened our doors in June 1979 and have worked hard, meeting many interesting people over the years. Jim, a snappy dresser, single with no siblings or children, quickly became friends with Neil even though he was forty years his senior. As their friendship grew, Jim moved into one of the upstairs rooms at our Inn. With fondness, we referred to him as our house detective. Aside from Jim, the rest of the rooms were rented by people on vacation in this pristine area.

On this beautiful day, three gentlemen walked into our bar and requested a table outside on the deck. The dining room was busy, so I decided to handle their lunch order by myself. I led them to the deck, sat them at a table with a lovely view of the lake and handed them menus.

Within minutes I was back at their table asking what they would like to order for lunch. A feeling of pleasure washed over me as I watched our business doing so well. Neil and I were fortunate to own a successful restaurant.

I walked into the kitchen and slapped the dupe under the bell, yelled to Neil that I had an order up, and returned to the bar. One of my usual barflies entered our establishment and I poured him his favorite beer and returned to the deck to engage myself in light conversation with the three men as I delivered their drinks. They were strangers, but after many years of waiting tables, I knew being friendly was important.

Excusing myself to see if their food was ready, I returned to the kitchen only to find that it would be a few more minutes before I could pick up their order. Back at the bar my regular customer was still sipping his beer. Everyone else was busy tending to our patrons, as I stood and chatted with my one customer at the bar. I hated when I had nothing to do. The kitchen bell rang and off I went to deliver lunch to my only three customers. They were pleased with their lunch and my service. When I returned to the bar, my customer was gone, his beer glass empty with a small gratuity lying on the bar.

Without any warning, a buzzing sound resonated in my ears and I rubbed my forehead hoping the fog would clear. A dark, lightless tunnel surrounded me and the walls closed in. The feeling was impossible to shake off, as my feet found their way to the ladies room.

As I slammed the door shut, I stared at my face in the mirror. "Go away!" I shouted to no one. I knew I had to get out of there.

Fear crept up my spine. I knew I was in trouble but I

just stood at the bar, like a statue unable to function. While staring at the cash register, nothing made any sense. Money was strewn everywhere. Somewhere in the deep recesses of my mind I knew I was supposed to be taking care of all of these checks with money on them, but I was unable to do so. The dark tunnel was closing in. As hard as I tried I could not climb out.

"Linda?"

The voice sounded familiar. It came from one of our longtime employees.

"Are you okay?"

My mouth could form no words. Time and space had shifted, leaving me in a strange new world. The employee ran to the kitchen and returned with Neil.

"Linda, what is wrong?" Neil asked, while looking into my eyes. His voice echoed in my brain, but I could not reply right away.

"Call the ambulance," Neil snapped at an employee. He led me to a table, pulled out a chair, and had me sit. The ambulance arrived in a timely manner. Someone, I don't remember who, put me on a stretcher. My last recollection was staring into the faces of people trying to help me. I surrendered to the darkness.

Luminescent lights shone above my head. A tray of sterile instruments gleamed beside my bed. A long tube dangled from the IV stand to a needle in my arm. Nurses and doctors gathered around, while Neil stood in the background. A thick haze encircled my head

The doctor moved closer to me. "Do you know your name?" he asked.

"Flo Jo," I stated with a hint of insolence. "Where did that name come from?" I thought.

"Do you know where you are?"

"I'm not sure." Heaviness weighed upon my eyelids. The shadowy tunnel reached out and grabbed me again. I willingly succumbed to the darkness once more.

When I awoke the second time, things were much clearer. I recognized the stark surroundings of the emergency room and knew I had been there for awhile. Neil stood by my side. No words were spoken between us. His face was filled with worry, and fatigue prevented me from allaying his fears.

I recognized the doctor when he walked into the room. "What is your name?" he asked.

"Linda," I replied.

"Do you have any children?"

"Yes I have three boys."

"What are their names?"

"Eric, Kyle and Kevin."

"What is your husband's name?"

"Neil; and we have been married for quite some time. Could you please tell me what this is all about?"

"Well, Mrs. McGovern, it appears as though you've had a stroke, which triggered the seizure you had in the ambulance. Remarkably, you seem to have no neurological damage, but we'll need to keep you in the hospital a few days for observation and tests. Meanwhile, we'll get you to a room and you should rest."

After four days of hospital food and numerous tests, I was on my way home. A stroke, I wondered. How could I have had a stroke and be perfectly fine? This was a question I would repeatedly ask myself over and over for the next few weeks. But for now I would follow the doctor's orders. I began to walk two miles a day.

August quickly slipped into September. A rash developed all over my body and was attributed to the seizure medication. My neurologist suggested I stop taking it.

"Linda," he said, "I truly think your stroke triggered your 'episode,' so the chances of you having another one are slim. But you must be seizure free for six month before you can drive again."

I was already walking everywhere and the little convertible Neil had bought for me sat outside in our driveway. I longed to be behind the wheel again.

The weather was perfect. Every day throughout September remained sunny, with a slight chill in the air. A true appreciation of our quaint little village took me by surprise as I walked and walked. Things I never noticed before now inundated me with their beauty. I noticed the little streams flowing by the side of the road, wisps of clouds in the sky, birds chirping, and pine trees reaching up to the heavens with majestic mountains as the backdrop. How did this escape me before?

September 28, 2003, exactly eight weeks after my seizure—or my stroke, as the doctor had called it—began with a feeling of gloominess both outside and within me. Rain poured down in buckets, filling the streets with puddles a child would be delighted to splash in. The question bounced back and forth in my head. Did I really want to walk a mile to the Inn through the pouring rain? Fatigue washed over me like the rain spilling its drops outside. After a multitude of sunny days, fetching an umbrella and walking to work seemed ludicrous.

Through the heavy precipitation, I saw her, sitting in the driveway, raindrops bouncing off of her roof. She was a thing of beauty to me. After not being behind her wheel for quite some time, I anticipated the freedom she could bring to me once again. Before I knew what I was doing, I was in the driver's seat.

The steering wheel felt alien as the key started the ignition. What could possibly go wrong? It had been two months since my so-called stroke and seizure. I would be fine. The Inn was only a mile away.

I reveled in the feeling she evoked in me. Memories flooded my mind of the many days flying down our country roads with the top down while listening to my favorite music. What could possibly be better than that? But for now, she was simply a necessary vehicle to get to work.

Fatigue continued to persist. Was it anxiety or was there really something wrong with me? Driving to the intersection, I made the left onto Route 8. My head felt woozy.

Pulling into the Inn's parking lot, I became conscious of feeling the same strange sensation I'd felt two months before. Trembling with fear, I put the car in park, but was unable to turn it off. The tunnel was grabbing me again. It seemed longer and darker this time. After sitting for a moment, I became aware that my thoughts were slipping away. I had to force myself out of the car. My feet took me up the steps to the Inn and I pushed my way through the crowd of customers waiting to get a table for breakfast. The Inn was busy, but I didn't care. Panic stricken; my arms swung open the kitchen door, "Somebody help me," I cried. "It's happening again.

I opened my eyes. The room was brightly lit. My body

tried to roll over, but wires hooked to my chest stopped me, and the IV in my arm pinched. I was conscious of the antiseptic odor permeating the room. Where was I? There was a hint of remembrance that I had been here before. What had happened?

SYNCHRONICITY

On September 8, three weeks before my second incident, Neil and I had been invited to a wine tasting party at my friend's home. Our hostess was born in France and her husband was a prominent physician. Among the guests there were several doctors and medical professionals.

This would be my first real outing since my first seizure and I was excited. Nothing could deter me from going. I had been taking French at our local community college for two years. My next step was to join the French club and I managed to convince Neil to attend these social gatherings. Speaking French had become my passion.

I mingled with the guests, drank some fine wine and immersed myself in a French environment. At first, I felt bad for Neil, since all of this was alien to him, but he managed to meet a gentleman who spoke French, but this kind man was happy to converse in English. They talked endlessly about golf and their love of the sport. Watching them banter back and forth helped me to relax and enjoy the afternoon. I lingered with my French-speaking comrades, and Neil seemed content. The hours passed quickly, and as we said our goodbyes, he placed a kiss upon my lips. "I truly enjoyed myself, Linda. Your friends are intriguing. It was a lovely afternoon."

"So you had a good time?" I asked.

"Yes," he replied, "I met this very engaging gentleman. He is a prominent neuro radiologist at Albany Med and he loves to play golf. I hope to have the chance to play with him sometime.

Driving home, reveling in the pleasant day we just experienced, the effects of this brief encounter affecting our lives in the near future, never entered my mind. Why would it? I had no idea at the time what was going to happen to me.

Do you believe in those meaningful coincidences that occur in your life? The ones you don't take notice of at the time. But when you reflect back, they almost seem like miracles or divine intervention. I believe, because it happened for me. Einstein once said coincidence is God's way of remaining anonymous.

After waking up in the hospital room, I saw Neil standing beside me. He looked as if someone had punched him in the stomach. As he regained his composure, I felt him lean over me. Wrapping his arms around my body, trying to avoid all the wires and tubes, he hugged me tight. "Linda, they say you have a brain tumor. We're going to St. Peter's Hospital to see a team of neurosurgeons. Hopefully they can help us.

I just wanted to go home. Nothing else seemed to matter. All of this was sickening to me. If I was going to die, I needed to be surrounded by all of the things I

cherished. My children were a huge concern for me. How would they react to this news? Will they miss me? How would Neil manage? He didn't know where all of our important papers were. Things needed to be put in order so he would be okay. What would happen to Kevin, our twenty two year old severely disabled little boy?
Who would take care of him as well as I had all these years? A million questions ran through my mind. No fear or anger, just questions.

St. Peter's Hospital was a nightmare. I shared a room with a young girl just coming out of brain surgery. Her pain was highly evident, and most of the night was spent listening to her cries of anguish. I retreated into my own deep thoughts about death and tried not to be afraid. Of course that was easier said than done. I put my life in God's hands.

Morning arrived slowly and Neil appeared along with the doctor. My roommate had finally fallen asleep so the room was quiet—except for the screaming fear raging inside my head. I was sure everyone could hear it, but no one seemed to notice.

The doctor approached my bed. "You can get dressed, Mrs. McGovern."

I looked to Neil and back.

"We're going to discharge you," the doctor said.

"Why?" I asked.

Neil sat on the bed and gripped my hand. The doctor finally met my eyes. "I'm sorry, but we can't operate. The tumor is too close to the motor strip that controls the right side of your body. Our technology is simply not sophisticated enough to perform this operation.

He waited for me to react. He waited for my shock, my

anger, my fear. He waited for me to cry or scream. But I did nothing he expected. Instead I smiled. I was going home to be with my children and to sleep in my own bed. Nothing else mattered.

Neil and I walked hand in hand to the car, each of us lost in our own thoughts, not uttering a word. I welcomed the warmth of the sun shining upon my face and had a new appreciation for the beauty of this day. I was so happy to be gone from that place of illness and dying. The sun's rays danced upon my face.

As Neil pulled out of the parking lot, he glanced over at me and said," Linda, I can't accept this diagnosis. I have an idea. Sit back and relax. I know this has been a rough few days for you. Close your eyes for awhile. I have to go see someone."

The warmth of the sun through the car's window was just what I needed, but I wondered how many more days I would have to enjoy life. My mind quickly released that morbid thought.

Neil pulled into the parking lot of Albany Medical Center. "Linda, just wait in the car and rest. I'll be back shortly."

Now I was totally confused. "Where are you going?" I asked.

"I need to see Tom, the fellow I met at the wine tasting party. I want him to look at your x-rays. He is a well-known radiologist and specializes in this field," Neil explained, his voice thick with desperation. "Maybe he can help. We can't go home and wait for you to die."

I sat in the car and calmly waited. This whole ordeal was more upsetting to Neil than it was to me. I hated to see him so troubled. I was fully resigned to my diagnosis. I didn't want to die, but knew in my heart the day would eventually arrive. We are born to die. Most of us never think about it, but death stalks us at every corner. If we believe, then we should not be afraid. But I was afraid. If Neil honestly felt someone could help me then I would comply with whatever he suggested.

The hour passed swiftly. Neil returned with a glimpse of hope in his eyes. Sitting down beside me, a wide smile erupted on his face. "Linda, I went to see Tom. He was waiting for me with outstretched arms. Our good friends from the wine tasting party called him after hearing about your predicament. Being on the Board of Directors for the hospital does have its benefits at times.

"Why?" I asked. "What could Tom possibly do for me? What did he say?"

"He told me your situation is grave, but we should not sit back and accept it. We should go to a university setting where they have the latest technology for this sort of thing. He knows a renowned surgeon at NYU. We are to go home and wait for his call. It's very difficult for someone to get an appointment with this doctor, but Tom thinks he can set this up for us. But I need to know." He took my hand and stared deeply into my eyes. "Do you want to go through with this? It could be scary."

I knew God was with me as I found this glimmer of hope. I would do whatever it took to rid myself of this terrible invader. I wanted to live to see my unborn grandchildren.

We left the car and walked up the steps to our house. Upon opening the door we saw it. The blinking red light, flashing on the answering machine. Ignoring the light, I sat down and savored the comfort of my surroundings. My home was simple, but I had spent many years decorating, painting, wallpapering and making it warm and inviting. I was proud of what I had accomplished, and now felt a twinge of sadness at the thought of leaving this place. I wondered what heaven would be like.

Neil immediately pushed the button to the answering machine, as I was lost in my own thoughts, and listened to the messages. All the information that was to alter my life was on one little machine. Tom had accomplished what we had thought impossible. I was to see Dr. Patrick Kelly on Wednesday at NYU. I don't believe that God remains anonymous.

REFLECTIONS OF THE PAST

The time was near. I was going to see a world-renowned brain surgeon. My life began to look as if I was one of those characters in the tear jerking movies I loved to watch. It was all so surreal.

As I sat on the sofa, alone with my thoughts, I pondered about what had happened three years before. Was my illness a result of this incident that rocked my world? Only God could answer that question. The pain and horror of that day remained etched in my mind.

September 27, 2000. We awoke to the sound of Kevin laughing over the baby monitor. Kevin is severely disabled. At twenty years old he is totally dependent on us for his every need. We continue to change his diapers and spoon feed him every day. Yet he is the light of our lives. What he offers us in unconditional love is beyond words. Smiles and hugs are abundant when we are with him.

The sun was shining brightly through our bedroom window. The leaves were beginning to turn their colors. Autumn has always been my favorite time of year here in the mountains. The air is crisp, with a gentle breeze blowing the leaves to the ground. Once the colors peak, the mountainside appears as though nature has taken her palette and splashed the trees with all her reds, oranges and yellows. There is nothing more beautiful. I felt myself snuggling closer to Neil, and we both delighted in the giggles coming from our little boy.

"Are you going to get Kevin ready for school, or should I?" I asked.

"Neil didn't answer; he seemed distracted.

"I can do it if you want," I said, "but I was hoping to take a shower."

"What? Oh yeah, I can get Kevin. Go take your shower," he answered as if he was thinking of something else.

Several minutes later, I joined him in the kitchen and made us both a cup of tea. "So, what are your plans for today?" I eagerly asked.

"Well, they don't need me at the Inn today, so I'm going out of town to run some errands. I want to pick up the pumpkins and cornstalks to put outside. He sipped his tea. "I have a hospital board meeting tonight at seven o'clock. Remember? I'll be home late, so plan to have dinner alone."

"Okay," I replied. I was used to his involvement with the hospital, since he had become a board member a few years ago. He needed to attend many meetings. Having dinner alone was not unusual for me. Actually, I secretly enjoyed the solitude. Sometimes I felt I couldn't get enough of it. I did notice, however, that he was dressed unusually nice for a hospital meeting. Oh well, I thought, it must be a special meeting.

We kissed goodbye. My day was spent doing chores

and waiting for Kevin's arrival home from school. Kevin's caregiver had the day off, so when Kevin came home, I had him to myself. As the evening approached, I laid Kevin down to sleep and poured myself a glass of wine. While turning on the oven, the shrill sound of the phone ringing interrupted my quiet time. I wondered who it could be. I didn't feel like talking to anyone.

I heard Laurie's voice on the other end of the line. I was confused as to why she would be calling me. We worked together—in fact, I was her employer—but we rarely called each other for idle chit chat.

"I feel compelled to tell you something," Laurie said.

"What is it?" I asked.

"I'm tired of all of the gossip going around at the Inn about Neil and Susan. Everyone seems to think they're having an affair. And I find it ironic that today is her birthday and Neil is out of town again."

I hung up on her. My mind was reeling. Could this be true? He actually had been going out of town a lot lately, but I never thought twice about it. Had I been blind? Susan had moved in August. We were done with her. She was a lousy employee; even Neil thought so. This must be a mistake. She was only twenty-five years old. What could Neil possibly have in common with her? She wasn't even pretty. This had to be a lie.

Pacing back and forth, I was at a loss. My stomach was in knots. Dinner was put aside. Trying to remain calm, I decided to call the hospital. I felt like a sneak checking up on my husband, but I had to know. They would tell me if there was a meeting tonight.

I dialed the number as I stirred the rice I was preparing

for dinner. The receptionist answered. "Hello, this is Linda McGovern, and I am trying to contact my husband Neil McGovern. He should be at the board meeting."

"I'm sorry Mrs. McGovern, but there is no board meeting tonight.

My heart began to palpitate as I paced back and forth.

"Are you sure?" I asked. "He told me this is where he would be."

"Hold on. I will double check, but I am pretty sure there is no meeting."

"Thank you."

Five long minutes passed as I waited for her return. I was sure she must be mistaken. I was sure this must be some sort of mix up.

Her voice on the other end of the line rang loud and clear. "Mrs. McGovern there is no meeting tonight. I'm sorry I can't help you."

Panic set in and I was confused. He couldn't have lied to me. He'd never done this before. What should I think?

The dinner I prepared sat cold on the counter. Sitting by the window, looking out to our driveway, I waited for his return. Sleep eluded me, 1:00am, 2:00am, 3:00am and then finally 4:00am. I watched as the car pulled up to our home. I stood at the door, ready to pounce like a tiger waiting for its prey.

He leisurely walked up the driveway. "What are you doing awake at this hour?" he asked.

"I've been waiting for you," I replied with an anger I had never felt before.

"Why? What's wrong?" he asked.

"I had a very disturbing phone call tonight about you and Susan. Is it true? Are you having an affair?"

He stared at me.

"There was no board meeting, and now it's four in the morning and you are just arriving home. How do you explain that?"

"You called the hospital?" he demanded. "Why would you do that? What are you trying to do, embarrass me?" He looked at me with lying eyes.

"I've never questioned your whereabouts before, but this was different. I needed to know if you'd been honest with me. Obviously, you were not." He avoided my face. "Linda you are so wrong. The receptionist must have been mistaken—or maybe she was unaware of this meeting. The Colonial Board meetings don't take place at the hospital."

"Then how do you explain being out so late?" My mind was reeling as I began to doubt myself.

He was calm and self-assured as he answered my questions without hesitation.

"The meeting lasted longer than usual, and afterwards I stopped at my usual watering hole and got caught up with the guys. I assure you, I did nothing wrong—except staying out too late."

I knew in my heart he would never lie to me, and he had relayed his story so quickly and confidently. What should I believe? My pulse echoed in my ears.

"Go to bed! I stated emphatically. "We'll talk later."

He trudged up the stairs and I heard his body fall into bed. I couldn't sleep. I went into Kevin's room. His eyes lit up at the sight of me. For once his infectious laughter was not soothing my soul. I had more frightening things on my mind. Like a robot without emotion I dressed and fed Kevin. The bus arrived and off he went to school.

Neil's footsteps echoed on the stairs. Tears rolled down my face. There were no words between us. He walked out the door. I was exhausted and found myself crawling up the stairs to enter the bed we had shared for twenty-three years. I wondered if we would continue to do so.

As tired as I was, I still couldn't sleep. Everything seemed alien to me. Remembering I had a lunch date with a dear friend, I picked up the phone and dialed her number. She answered right away. "Diane," I said. "Something has come up and I can't make it to lunch today. I'm sorry."

"What's wrong?" she asked. "I can't talk about it now, but I will call you in a few days. Thanks for understanding."

My head was fuzzy from the lack of sleep. I dressed, got in my convertible and drove away. Cruising at a comfortable speed with the wind blowing through my hair, my head started to clear. There was no destination; just the wind, sun and my unbridled thoughts. Was he really at the meeting? Had he stayed out late with the guys? Could he be telling the truth?

Our marriage had been strong for twenty-three years, and nothing like this had ever happened before. My faith in him was rekindled.

As I neared the Inn, I saw the bus outside. He was catering a dinner for the leaf-peekers, a word we often used to describe tourists traveling through our area during the fall. I parked and went inside. He was busy, but I interrupted him. "When you get home, we need to talk." I turned to leave, but then faced him again. "I bought you a jug of apple cider."

He appeared to be distracted. "Thanks for the cider. I'll be home within the hour."

"I'll order a pizza." I said.

Arriving at home with pizza in hand and a positive attitude, I felt everything would be fine. We had drifted apart these past few years since my mother passed away, but now we would have the chance to fix what ailed us. I was convinced this was all there was to it. We needed to reconnect. Any suggestions Neil had would be welcomed with open arms. It might be difficult for me because I had never taken criticism well, but I would be a steadfast soldier and listen to what he had to say,

Kevin was asleep and our caregiver had retired to her apartment. I was alone. An hour passed before I heard the car pull into the driveway. The candles I lit flickered in the shadows as the sun started to set. Two plates, two wine glasses and a cardboard box of pizza completed the romantic setting. I was full of anticipation about what we would say to each other. Hopefully the conversation would reflect the ambience I tried to set. My anger had dissipated and I wanted us to rediscover what we seemed to have lost.

He walked through the door. Immediately, an unpleasant feeling washed over me. Something was wrong. The candles, wine and pizza were all a mistake. I could feel it. I braced myself, but never expected what was about to take place.

Neil slumped on the couch, ignoring the loving ambience set in the kitchen. "Sit down, Linda," he said. "I need to tell you something. I lied to you last night. You were right. I have been having an affair with Susan these past three months. I can't take it anymore—all the lying, deceit, and most of all the trusting look in your eyes. I am so sorry."

I couldn't breathe. The knife pierced my heart. Everything started to make sense. The endless nights alone, phone calls saying he couldn't drive home because he was too drunk, never seeing him before I went to bed, the constant trips to Albany; how could I have been so blind?

A low roar that escalated into a scream escaped my mouth. "How could you?" I screamed as my head spun. I wanted to throw up. Jumping out of my chair, I began to pound him with my fists. The inquisition began. My questions were abundant and not satisfactorily answered. He said he was sorry, but this was way beyond my comprehension.

"I love you, Linda. Can you ever forgive me? I don't want to lose you."

Forgiveness was the furthest thing on my mind. Escape was my only solution. I needed to leave. Looking at him made me sick.

The night was hell. The next morning I packed my bags and Neil drove me to the train station. I was in no shape to drive. The train arrived on time, and I never looked back. I was going home to Long Island, the place where I grew up. My sister, Barbara, would help me get through this. I craved the comfort and sympathy she could provide. Whether or not I would return was a question that hung in the air as Neil watched me board the train. My descent into the dark abyss began.

MY PAINFUL DECISION

Upon disembarking from the train, I saw Barbara waiting on the platform. She knew how to soothe my soul. She took me into her arms as my tears began and continued to flow.

As Barbara released her hold on me, she spoke in her most soothing tone. "I realize you are hurt, but this is not the end of the world. Worse things could happen. I'm surprised at what Neil has done, and you have every right to be angry. But I know him and he is a great guy."

"I don't think I am strong enough to endure this. I thought we had something special. But now it's ruined."

"You're going to have to make some tough decisions while you're here. Do you want to stay with him?" she asked. She stepped away from me. And then to my surprise she put her arms around me once more and told me she loved me. I was confused and wanted to answer her question immediately.

"I don't know right now. I do know I love him and always have. But how can I ever trust again and get past this terrible hurt?"

"Try not to think that way. He has made a terrible

mistake and you should try to forgive him. You said he told you he was sorry and you are the one he wants to be with. It could have been the other way around," she said gently.

I pulled back from her. "So you're telling me I should be grateful? That's absurd. I've done nothing wrong and he is supposed to get a pass on this?"

"Calm down, Sis. We'll work through it."

I sighed. "I'm way too confused. I need time to think without having to look at his face. Thanks for letting me stay with you."

Her words made me contemplate my situation. Should I stay with him? Or should I leave? Could I actually forgive this horrible betrayal of everything I believed in? I didn't know.

The roller coaster ride had begun.

After consuming one too many wines the previous night, Barbara and I took a drive to the ocean in the early morning. She knew how much I loved being there and wanted to give me some space. I sat for hours on the soft white sand, listening to the roar of the ocean's waves. A sense of peace entered my being. I needed to go home. Not right away, but soon. I had to face this alone.

Four days later, saying goodbye to Barbara was difficult. I felt safe and secure when I was with her, just like when we were children. Nothing could harm us. But now I'm grown up, my mother is gone, Barbara is married. I'm on my own. For the first time in my life, I felt vulnerable. I had no idea how I was going to handle this situation.

I boarded the train on a picturesque September

afternoon. I watched all the people coming and going, and wondered how many of them were truly happy. I wanted to scream out loud and tell them how hurt I was. My husband had betrayed me. Yet I remained silent. They didn't care and I knew that. I gazed out the window lost in my own misery and watched as the world passed by.

THE DARK ABYSS

The train arrived on time. Neil stood on the platform. Bile rose in my throat and I squelched the sick feeling in my stomach as I lent him a smile. He took me in his arms and my body went rigid as I considered my next few words.

"I'm home, but I'm not sure I should be here. I made up my mind to stay with you, but I can't promise that forgiveness will be on the horizon. And I know I will never forget. If you can live with that, then maybe we can work things out. But for now, you will have to prove a lot of things to me. My trust in you is broken; maybe with time I will regain it, but I'm not sure of anything. For now, I just want to go home and see Kevin."

We kissed and made up. At least he thought we did. The deep dark ache in my heart persisted. I went to counseling and reached out to my friends, but nothing seemed to help. How was I ever going to forgive and forget?

I began writing in my journal, recording every thought and feeling I experienced. But the past crept in, like a burglar in the night. We struggled to keep our relationship alive.

Barbara took me on a trip to Europe, with the hope that I would feel better. At any other time in my life I would have been overjoyed, but overwhelming sadness trailed behind me, until I found Paris. I fell in love with this magnificent city. The history and language enthralled me. Lying in bed in the Hotel Louvre, listening to the quiet breathing of my sister while she slept, a steely determination rose within me. When I returned home, I was going back to school to learn the French language. I would become a Francophile.

And I did. My classes were great. My professor was fun and he made learning easy. I enjoyed these classes immensely, and while I was there all my troubles seemed to dissipate. I enrolled in the local French Club. Our trips to Montreal were wonderful.

But real life ensued. Neil and I fought, and I struggled to keep my feelings at bay. My mouth got the better of me, blurting out accusations and hurtful remarks. I fought a battle with an unknown enemy. My words were razor-sharp and hard to control. Sinking like a ship, I knew I was in trouble. Someone needed to help me. Despite all my prayers, I felt like God had forsaken me.

My daily journal overflowed with conflicting emotions—emotions even I didn't understand. One morning, after tossing and turning all night, I woke and noticed my journal sitting on the nightstand beside my bed. On each page, my words screamed out at me: you are making yourself sick; you are making yourself sick; you are making yourself sick. My strength waned.

I turned to God once more. The hole I was falling down seemed deeper and darker than before, and I didn't know how to climb out. In the darkness of the chasm, I saw the rope. As I clung to it and ascended the walls, my brain tumor appeared. "This is your way out," it said.

We packed our bags. New York City was five hours away. We made reservations at the Milford Plaza hotel. Not exactly the Ritz, but comfortable enough for me. Besides, I had other things on my mind, and hotel surroundings were not one of them.

I was full of apprehension, so we spent our night quietly watching TV. Neither of us spoke. I had the feeling his thoughts mirrored mine. Listening to the drone of the television, I closed my eyes and drifted off to another place. A place I had never been before. My mother and father were waiting. They looked happy and appeared to beckon me.

I was jolted from my sleep. Neil's body lay next to mine; sweat dotted my forehead. Was this where I was going? Would I be joining my parents soon? As I lay beside Neil, the gentle rhythm of his snoring helped allay my fears. I was still alive; tomorrow would determine my fate.

Morning finally arrived with the blaring resonance of traffic, police sirens and ambulances. A far cry from the birds chirping outside my window at home. Looking down upon all of the commotion these few city blocks could emit, I had a strange feeling. Should I be here? Could this doctor help me?

NYU was a massive labyrinth of hallways leading to many doors. People scurried about like rats trapped in a maze. I followed Neil, lagging behind, carrying my MRI report and x-rays. His pace quickened as he recognized the hallway leading to the doctor's office.

"Why are you walking so fast? I can't keep up." I realized how hesitant I was to see the doctor.

"We're going to be late, and the sooner this is over with, the better. We're very lucky to have this appointment, and we should be on time."

We, I thought. *What's this we stuff? I'm the one with the brain tumor. He's acting like this is happening to him. I don't even want to be here.*

But I was stuck. I always follow the rules. Feeling like I wanted to crawl under a rock and shut out the world, I managed to put on my bravest face. We entered his office. I glanced around the room, taking notice of all the people sitting and waiting. No one looked very sick, but the anguish was evident on their faces.

As a wave of anxiety washed over me, Barbara and my sister-in-law Moe sat quietly, speaking in a hushed tone.

"What are you guys doing here?" I asked. "You shouldn't have taken a day off from work just to be with me."

"We wanted to support you in your time of need," they replied in unison.

Tears rolled down my cheeks and the taste of salt flavored my lips. Two people I love dearly were by my side. Maybe this wouldn't be so bad.

"Linda McGovern," the receptionist bellowed. I hesitated, but rose from my chair and went to face the music. Neil followed. Barbara and Moe wished me good luck.

The doctor sat in his leather chair with an elfish grin upon his face. He was jovial, but matter of fact as he introduced himself. He could have been Kris Kringle's double from *Miracle on 34th Street.*

He took my x-rays, which were now clammy from resting in my sweaty palms, and put them up to the light. He spoke without any hesitation. "I see what needs to be done. You need to be back here on Monday for a series of tests. They will not be pleasant, but if I can locate the exact spot of the tumor and perform a biopsy, we might have a chance."

There was that *we* stuff again. Wasn't this a *me* thing? All of a sudden a light bulb went on in my head. This was a *we* thing. I couldn't possibly do this alone. Of course, it was my life they were toying with, but I needed all the help I could get. The possibility that I could die kept creeping into my skull

Barbara and Moe were sitting patiently, waiting for some news. "What did he say?" they both asked.

"I'm really not sure. It was just too much information for me to absorb, or maybe I didn't really want to. I allowed my mind to wander to my favorite place. While listening to Neil relay the news, I found myself floating on a raft in the Caribbean. Palm trees swayed gently with the breeze. From my raft I could see the beach bar. The Pina Colada tasted cool and refreshing in my mouth. This is where I belonged.

"Linda!" he shouted. "We're leaving now. Barbara and Moe would like to go out to lunch. Are you hungry?"

"What? Oh sure! I would love to have lunch. I'm so glad you came, but I'm sorry you made this trip for nothing. There seems to be no solution."

Moe stood up and laughed out loud. "Linda, did you

not hear a word Neil has told us? The doctor said you need to be back on Monday for some tests and a biopsy. There's a good chance this tumor is benign. Let's just wait and see."

I was dizzy with frustration. I had a brain tumor. No matter what anyone said, this couldn't be good. I wanted to escape, but didn't know how or where to go. Lunch with some lighthearted banter was not what I was looking for.

As we walked down the streets of New York, I felt myself pulling away from the three of them. I tried desperately to seem happy, but my effort was fruitless. The words "brain tumor" reverberated in my head. I was finally able to admit to myself that I was scared. I followed obediently like a puppy dog, not involved with any of the conversation. Once again I was lost in my own reverie. I could not face the truth.

THE TWILIGHT ZONE

On our way back home I tried not to think about Monday. I stared out the car window, then turned to Neil and asked him again. "So what exactly did the doctor say? Should I be afraid?"

"You have every right to be afraid, but try not to be. The doctor said you need to undergo some tests and if he can locate the tumor, he will perform a biopsy, and of course you'll be sedated," he said. I must've still looked blank, as he continued in a patient voice, as though explaining something to a child in kindergarten. "First, you'll undergo some tests with a halo on your head. I'm not sure what that entails, but you'll have another MRI, CT scan, and an angiogram of your brain. These tests will determine if the doctor can locate the exact position of the tumor. We won't know much more until they are completed. Try not to worry about it. You'll be fine."

But I wasn't fine. I was scared to death. I was drowning in medical muck and mire. My mind focused on one thing; my favorite gambling haunt.

"Neil, when we get home, will you take me to the casino? I need a few hours to escaped, and playing the slots is the perfect answer. When I'm there I think of nothing else. Would you humor me?"

"Of course I will. Tomorrow, after Kevin goes to school, we'll go gambling. I'd love to see you relax." He gave me a smile. "But remind me to call our health insurance. We need to have a referral."

The next day, Neil dropped me off at the casino, claiming he had errands to run. We would meet for dinner at eight o'clock. The ringing bells from the slot machines were a warm welcome. Sitting down to the machine I preferred, I became absorbed in the world of gambling. Win, lose, win, lose.......never risking too much money, helped me to forget my cares. People all around me were having fun and before I realized the time, I heard someone mention it was 8:15. *Oh my God,* I thought, *I hope Neil isn't angry because I'm late.*

At the end of the long corridor, I saw Neil standing with cell phone in hand. His face was beet red and he was pacing back and forth. The anger on his face was evident. I knew I was fifteen minutes late, but I never thought he would be mad at me. As I approached, he waved me off, deep in conversation with someone. I stood there, shuffling my feet, feeling guilty that I had made him wait. His anger was escalating, as I realized this phone call had nothing to do with my tardiness.

He flipped the lid of the phone closed, turned to me, and said, "Let's go."

"What?" I asked. "I thought we were going to have dinner."

"I'm too upset to eat. This has been the worst evening for me."

He pulled me to the bench alongside the window and told me to sit down. "Linda, I need to know one thing. Do you really want to go through with this? It's imperative I know how you feel."

"What are you talking about? Of course I don't want to but I have to. Is there any other choice?" I looked at him. "Should I just sit back and allow myself to die, without putting up a fight? Yes, I need to go to NYU and do what they tell me, but I'm scared. Why are you asking me this?"

"The insurance company is denying our claim. They told me you could be treated locally, even though our local hospital won't treat you. Since this is Columbus Day weekend, it seems the paperwork has not gone through. We'll have to use our credit card on Monday to pay the doctor ten thousand dollars required for the biopsy. And God only knows what the hospital will cost."

I stared at him.

"It's all happening so fast, and I just needed to know if you really wanted to do this."

I thought for a few moments about the situation. Was I now going to bankrupt my family? Anger welled up inside me. For years we had been paying for health insurance, never using it, and at this critical moment in my life, they were telling me they wouldn't pay. This was an injustice. Damn them! They were not going to influence my decision. If we had to max out our credit cards, then so be it. I wanted the chance to live.

I turned to Neil. "I need to do this. I'm sorry I'm causing so much trouble."

Confusion overwhelmed me. *Was he hoping I would say no?*

"That's all I needed to hear. I know you're scared. I was just afraid I was pushing you into a frightening situation." He gave me a tight smile. "But knowing you have the courage to endure what will happen is all I needed to hear. I will fight the insurance company. They can't get away with this."

We never had dinner. The drive home found us with nothing to say. My fun day was over and now reality set in. In two days we would be on our way to New York City where my voyage into the Twilight Zone would begin.

It still seems surreal. I have no idea what compelled me to agree to go through a day of pure hell. Someone or something must have influenced me. Or maybe I was very naïve.

Darkness was upon us as we arrived at the hotel on Sunday night, the day before my ordeal. We were two blocks from NYU. Our room was lovely with a spectacular view of the East River and the city lights. At any other time I would have enjoyed this room immensely. Neil spared no expense.

I gazed out the window, butterflies dancing in my stomach. I had agreed to spend ten thousand dollars on something I didn't want. There was no turning back. I had to be brave, and yet I was not feeling the least bit courageous. I climbed into bed, then tossed and turned while listening to the gentle rhythm of Neil's snoring. The night was endless.

I laid my head upon the pillow, terrified of the impending morning.

The alarm clock pierced my brain and I turned it off. "Neil, I said gently, "You need to wake up. We have a half hour to get to the hospital."

"How did you sleep?" he asked.

"Just fine," I replied as I wiped the sweat from my forehead. I couldn't help but lie. The day was going to be long enough. He didn't need to worry about my fatigue. This was becoming my own private battle.

We dressed comfortably and left the hotel. The cloak of darkness didn't help to allay my fears. My knees buckled as I lagged behind, trying desperately to put off the inevitable. These were the two longest blocks I had ever walked. Having Neil by my side lent me some comfort.

We knew where to go this time. I was amazed by the amount of people scurrying about in the wee hours of the morning. Once we arrived, tons of paperwork needed to be filled out, so I sat in the waiting room, rested the papers on my lap, and concentrated on the questions.

Upon finishing this tedious chore, I gazed around the room, trying to figure out what most of the people were here for. Did they all have brain tumors? Mindlessly staring, as I was, lost in my own thoughts, I felt a tap on my shoulder. Turning around, I saw my sister-in-law, Moe standing beside me. Her presence comforted me, even though her words didn't help to dispel my apprehension.

"Linda, don't be scared. Everything will be just fine. NYU is an excellent hospital, and this doctor knows what he is doing. You need to relax, and before you know it, this will be over."

I just shrugged. I knew in my heart this day was just the beginning of a long journey. I've always believed that fate is pre-determined. I was in God's hands, and most of all, my neurosurgeon.

Waiting was the hardest part. We chatted as I kept glimpsing at the receptionist, waiting for my name to be called. Concentrating on small talk was difficult.

"Linda McGovern. We're ready for you. Follow me."

I entered a room similar to an operating room and became alarmed. Then I remembered. I needed to be under anesthesia for the halo to be put on my head. But I wondered why. It was just some metal contraption to keep my head still. Why anesthesia? The doctor's explanation of this procedure was difficult to recall.

My body welcomed the drug, but in what seemed like only a few minutes, I was awake and feeling fine. Neil and Moe stood close by my side.

'That wasn't so bad," I said. And then my head moved. A pain more excruciating than anything I had ever felt shot through my temple. "What is this?"

"Linda, don't you remember the doctor telling you about this? You must keep perfectly still. There are four screws in your skull holding the halo in place. This is necessary for the doctor to perform the tests to pinpoint the tumor. In a couple of hours they'll remove the halo and you'll be able to rest."

I looked at Neil as he spoke. The anesthesia was wearing off and the throbbing began. A tear rolled down my cheek, but I couldn't wipe it away and no one noticed. They said just a couple of hours. Okay, I could do this. At least I thought I could.

I lay perfectly still. The slightest movement shot searing bolts of pain through my head. The ceiling was my only view. People talked to me, but I ignored them as I waited patiently for the first test. I knew it would be an MRI. I'd had them previously after my seizures, so I wasn't nervous. I knew I could tolerate the test as long as no one asked me to move.

As we waited in the hall outside the x-ray room, Neil and Moe tried to cheer me up. Laughing was painful, so I just lay on the gurney listening to their jokes. Humor wasn't my strongest point at that moment.

The technician wheeled me into the x-ray room. MRI's are not pleasant, but I was comfortable with the test. Forty-five minutes later, I was done. I couldn't see them, but I knew Neil and Moe were following behind. They were with me every step of the way.

More time passed as I continued to stare at the ceiling. Someone had to be driving nails into my head. The pain was constant and unrelenting. Too tired to complain, I quietly endured the throbbing ache in my skull.

The gurney started to move. The attendant said it was time for the CT scan. I was being wheeled through massive hallways, on my way to another test. Catching a glimpse of myself in a window, I was horrified. The image of Frankenstein stared back at me. At least this will be over soon.

We entered the room with the ominous machine looming in the background. I wasn't scared. CT scans are easy. But this time was different. I needed to actually sit up to get on the table, but realized I couldn't. Bolts of lightning were shooting behind my eyes as the nurse lifted me up. The tears began and were uncontrollable.

"I can't do this. I'm in too much pain. I need some drugs. How do you expect anyone to endure this torture? Please help me."

"Calm down, Mrs. McGovern. We'll be done with this test in a minute."

A minute wasn't fast enough.

"If you think this is uncomfortable, wait until you have the angiogram," the nurse added. "That test takes over an hour. Just try to relax."

I couldn't believe what I was hearing. Throbbing, pounding pain continued. Was I a coward?

The CT scan was quick but very uncomfortable. I was happy to be away from Nurse Ratchet. My gurney was rolled out into the hallway once again as we waited for the final exam. The angiogram was next. I had no idea what this entailed and didn't care. All I wanted was some pain killers. But none were to be had.

I was drifting in and out of reality. Neil and Moe spoke to me, but I couldn't comprehend their words. The pain was becoming more and more unbearable. There was no relief in sight. As I lay on the gurney, fading in and out, I started to recall when I was a child and I would watch episodes of the Twilight Zone; a television show that was bizarre and unreal. Yet the fear that show evoked in me was now the same fear I was experiencing.

The technicians came to get me. Tears rolled down my face and I became frantic.

"Help me!" I pleaded. "I can't bear this anymore. Please don't make me go through with this."

White coats surrounded me. A calm soothing voice spoke. "Mrs. McGovern, I realize you are in a tremendous amount of discomfort, but I assure you we'll make you as comfortable as possible." A hand rested on my shoulder. "This test will take about an hour, and drugs cannot be used during this exam—we need you cogent. Just relax and allow us to put you in a position that won't cause you any more pain."

I refused to believe him. The previous nurse had just told me if I thought I was distressed with the CT scan, then I would be even more distressed with the angiogram. I begged once more for some drugs. My head was about to explode.

Neil and Moe were in another room. The voice I had heard before spoke again.

"Linda, we're going to situate you on this bed and put your head into a position that should alleviate your discomfort. Unfortunately, you'll have to lift up in order for us to do this. I promise you, once we have you still and ready for the angiogram, you should feel better. Are you aware of what we're about to do? This test takes at least an hour, as it's a delicate procedure. We need to cut your femoral artery and insert tubing up through your body and into your brain. You really shouldn't feel any pain, but you must lie perfectly still. Once the tube is in place, we'll shoot some dye into the tube and take pictures. Really quite simple when you think about it. You just need to be quiet and keep perfectly still."

Simple, I thought. Dying would be easier. But I didn't want to die.

Once they moved me and my head was in place, I couldn't believe how true to his word he was. The throbbing continued, but the searing, driving force of nails pounding my skull ceased. The tension left me and for once I was able to relax.

I continued to stare at the ceiling. The technician kept me engaged in smooth conversation, so I never felt the knife cut my artery. These people were true professionals. They knew how to distract me form what was happening. For the first time in hours, I was comfortable.

"Okay, the tubing is in place. Now we'll inject the dye. You might taste it and feel a warm sensation throughout your body. Don't worry, this can't hurt you. When I tell you to, I want you to keep your eyes closed and don't open them until I say so. This is imperative. Do you understand?"

"Sure. I can do that. I'm not afraid."

"Good girl. Now close your eyes and don't open them until I tell you to."

I did as he said. My eyes were shut tight. Within a matter of seconds, the most spectacular light show appeared behind my eyes. Every blood vessel in my brain lit up like neon lights. I was amazed and didn't want it to end. I felt like I had just taken an electrifying walk through my brain. It was an astounding experience.

"Open your eyes, Linda. We're going to do this again. Are you ready?"

"Yes I am." And I shut my eyes for the second time.

This time I concentrated more on what I was seeing. Remarkable, overwhelming, splendid, were the thoughts running through my head. I now knew why doctors were fascinated by the brain. I got a secret glimpse of what is in there.

"Open your eyes. We're done. The pictures came out good. Do you feel alright?"

"Are you kidding? That was the most spectacular experience I've ever had. It was awesome."

They all laughed and I wondered what was so funny.

They replied in unison. "You're the first person who has ever proclaimed an angiogram to be awesome. We're glad you enjoyed it."

"I could do this all night. The whole procedure was fascinating. Thank you for being so nice."

Another orderly entered the room. An incredibly handsome face was standing beside me. My eyes were focused on him as I began to wonder what he was here for. His face was filled with kindness as he started to speak. "Linda, I am here to remove the tubing that had been inserted in your artery for the angiogram. I now need to compress the wound."

What do you mean?" I asked.

"Well, we just cut one of your major arteries to the heart and brain, and compressing the wound is better than stitching it. I will have to press very hard for about twenty minutes. I'm sorry, because I know this will be painful."

He was right. It hurt. I didn't say anything as he continued to apply pressure to my wound. I lay perfectly still as he did his job. His hands were large but his eyes were soft with compassion. Finally the job was done.

"Linda, I'm sorry if I hurt you, but now it is imperative that you lay perfectly still. We don't want the wound to open up again. Any movement could cause that to happen. Someone will be in soon to take you to another room. Just relax and try not to move."

"Another room?" I asked. "I thought I would be going in for my brain biopsy. Isn't that the protocol?"

"I'm sorry. Didn't anyone tell you? Your surgeon had to perform an emergency surgery and we're not sure when he'll be done. Meanwhile, you'll be taken to a room upstairs to wait for your biopsy. Someone should have told you." And then he was gone.

Neil and Moe entered the room where I lay perfectly still, concerned that the wound might start bleeding. The throbbing in my head persisted. My leg was sore. But the worst was yet to come. They would soon be drilling a hole in my skull to perform a biopsy. How long would I have to wait?

Neil looked at me with adoration in his eyes. "Linda, you were amazing. I can't believe you went through that test and never complained. I don't think I could have done it."

"Oh I have many complaints, but they're not worth talking about. I'm suffering terribly. Please have someone get this halo off my head. I'm not sure I can bear it any longer. You need to find out what is going on. I'm begging you."

He left the room and Moe stood by my side. Blinded by the pain I was unaware of anyone else's existence. She understood. Her quiet presence helped to calm me, but the hammering in my head would not cease.

The clock continued to tick away the minutes which soon turned into hours. Neil returned to inform me that the doctor was unavailable until he was out of surgery. This meant I had to continue to suffer the excruciating pain from the halo on my head. I lay still unable to shed a tear.

The gurney started to move. Some nurse was pushing me to a new place where the
ceiling looked different. There was a curtain drawn to separate me from the other patient lying in bed. The nurse spoke, "Mrs. McGovern, we're going to have you wait here in this hospital room until the doctor can see you. We're not sure how long his surgery will last. His patient is in critical condition. Since he is the one to remove your halo, you'll have to rest here until he's finished. Try to relax."

The urge to cry came over me, but I managed to suppress the feeling. Neil and Moe stood in the room, both at a loss for words. No more jokes, no more pats on the back, just deep worry etched on their faces as they observed my suffering.

"Go away, both of you! Why don't you go get something to eat? Moe, I know you must be longing for a cigarette. I'll be fine. There's nothing to do but wait."

They both hesitated before finally agreeing to leave me alone. But I wasn't by myself. Out of the corner of my eye I could see the curtain that separated me from the person in the other bed. The sound of vomiting was unpleasant and I wondered what was wrong with her. Muted voices talked about thyroid cancer. For a brief second I forgot my own pain and wondered what she must be going through. My heart went out to her. As my head throbbed, I realized there are people with worse problems. I needed to start being brave and fight harder for my life. My suffering would end. I could quietly endure my situation.

Neil and Moe returned as I silently prayed to God. We didn't talk. The hours seemed
like an eternity. Finally the clock said 5:30, almost twelve hours since they first screwed the Frankenstein halo into my head. I heard the clicking of heels coming down the hallway. My headache was now intolerable. The hammer and nails kept pounding in my skull. There was no more thinking, just silent agony.

The men in white entered my room, almost looking like angels coming to rescue me. The wheels of the gurney rolled once again. *Oh my God!* I thought. *Where are we going now?*

"Mrs. McGovern. We're taking you down to the OR.

You'll wait in the hallway until the doctor comes out to see you. He should be here soon. It's almost over. Good luck with everything."

The gurney came to a halt. The attendants left me in the hallway, waiting for the doctor. Neil held my hand and told me I was almost done. I couldn't move my head, so I gestured with my hand for him to lean closer. Trying not to cry, I asked if he could find someone to give me painkillers. I was at the end of my rope. He told me there was no one to ask for pain relief. A loud scream formed in my throat but did not come out. I remained silent.

The doctor appeared. I felt his hand upon my shoulder, as he apologized for the long ordeal I had endured. He was very jovial, unlike me. The results of the tests were plopped upon my stomach, and he told me he had a change of plan. The tumor had been located and instead of a biopsy, a full craniotomy would be the next step. His confidence took me by surprise. In a matter of seconds I was supposed to make one of the most crucial decisions of my life.

"I need your permission to do the full surgery. If you would like, I can still do the biopsy, but I'm positive I can get this tumor out. I realize what a surprise this is, but I feel the craniotomy would be the best move. Is this okay with you?"

Neil and Moe nodded. They both agreed, but it was up to me. Hesitating for just a few minutes, I looked into the doctor's eyes and told him he could perform the surgery only if someone gave me drugs immediately. I could not wait another moment. Someone had to alleviate the pounding in my head.

As I contemplated my decision, someone held my

hand. I knew it wasn't Neil because I felt the warmth of his touch on my left side. The reassuring grip I felt was in my right hand, yet no one was there. At that moment I knew for sure that a guardian angel was by my side. I was certain of my choice.

"If you get someone to get me some drugs to relieve the pain, I will consent to the surgery. I don't care what you do, as long as you get this damn halo off my head."

The doctor chuckled. I watched him swing open the doors, and before I knew it, a young anesthesiologist dressed in flowered scrubs moved toward me with a huge smile.

"Hello, Linda. I'm Dr. Feel Good. Within minutes you're going to forget all that you've been through. I have the perfect drugs."

And that is the last thing I recalled.

RECOVERY

I was drowning. No, I was choking. I couldn't breathe. Flailing my arms, unable to speak, someone finally noticed my distress.

"Oh my goodness. She's awake. Get that tube out of her throat."

I gasped for air as they removed the device for intubation during surgery. Relief washed over me as air flowed freely through my lungs. Dozens of interns stayed close by me, and I wondered why I was here in this brightly lit room full of medical equipment. Then I saw my doctor and it all came back to me. I was alive. They had opened my skull, operated on my brain, and I was still here. A feeling of calm washed over me as I remembered the hand I'd felt gripping mine. Someone had walked hand in hand with me through this whole ordeal.

The following events are still a little hazy for me, but I distinctly recall being wheeled out of the OR into recovery. Everything was clear, and my most dominant thought was that I had survived brain surgery. I felt like singing, and I did. As the tight bandage wrapped around my head, squeezed my eyes, I spotted Neil and Moe. I started to laugh and belted out the tune from *Lady and the Tramp*. "I am Siamese if you please. I am Siamese if you don't please." I couldn't have been happier as I noticed the look of relief in Neil's eyes. He and Moe laughed uncontrollably, almost hysterically, as a release from all the tension they had endured for four hours, waiting to see if I would be okay.

The nurse ushered them out of the recovery room. "You can see her in the morning. She needs to rest. We'll keep a close eye on her. Go home and get some rest yourselves."

I felt the light kiss upon my cheek, and then they were gone. I needed to sleep, but every time I drifted off, my eyes would pop open and look at the clock. Only ten minutes had gone by. This continued throughout the night. The nurse checked on me every so often, and I had no complaints. There were other people in much more distress than me. In fact, I didn't even have a headache.

Morning arrived with Neil by my side. Another MRI was planned for me. Lying in the hallway, waiting for the test, my sister appeared and I was so happy to see her.

After the MRI, I was taken to a room with a terrific view of the East River. Another woman shared the same room but the divider made the room seem private enough. Barbara and Neil sat by my side. Fatigue crept in. My eyelids were heavy and sleep overtook me.

For the next four days, I rested quietly in bed. The bandage around my head was annoying but otherwise I had no pain. Tylenol wasn't even necessary. My roommate was a different story. She'd had a tummy tuck and was writhing in pain. It was difficult for me to muster up any empathy for her, since she chose to have this done for her own vanity. I had brain cancer. Sympathy seemed to find its way out the door. Her cries of pain were hard to listen to.

Every morning the troops, along with my doctor, marched into the room, like a gaggle of geese following their leader. Six a.m. was an awful hour to answer questions, but I managed. He instructed his entourage about my tumor and asked what they would do if confronted with this same situation. I was fascinated. *So this is how they learn,* I thought. *I hope they can be as good as this doctor someday.*

Friday finally arrived. I was being discharged. My excitement at the prospect of going home escalated. My desire to see Kevin and be able to sleep in my own bed overwhelmed me. I never lost sight of the fact that I was lucky to be going there.

Upon my discharge many orders were being given. Stay on seizure meds, don't wash your hair, rest, no sex, but most of all don't lift anything heavy. He told me my prognosis was good, but we had to wait and see the pathology report.

"You'll have to return on Wednesday to have your staples removed and determine the next step. Go home and rest. So far, you're doing very well. Slowly wean off the steroids like I told you. I'll see you next week."

I dressed in a hurry, covered my head with a scarf to hide the pressure bandage, and with a skip in my step, left the hospital. Even the city air smelled good. Neil suggested I try to sleep during the five hour drive back home, but I was too elated to relax. I was going home. I drank in the sunshine, blue sky, and for once looked forward to seeing the mountains.

NIGHTMARES CAN COME TRUE

I was home, but knew I had to be back in the city on Wednesday. Plans were made with my caregiver so she could watch Kevin while we were gone once again. A good friend had offered her mother's apartment for us to stay in while we were in the city. Hotel rooms were becoming expensive and we were grateful to be in a homey atmosphere.

We arrived on Tuesday and settled in. I was tired but hungry, so we ordered take-out. After watching TV, I quickly fell asleep. Tomorrow was a big day. The results would be in.

Waking in a strange bed was becoming commonplace. Hotels, hospitals and now someone's apartment seemed to be our protocol. When would I be able to go home and stay there?

The next day we drove out of New Jersey, over the George Washington Bridge, and took the FDR Drive along the east River, arriving at NYU. We were back in the massive building that had so far saved my life. If it wasn't for the gooey mess my hair had become, I could have easily forgotten the brain surgery. My spirits were high, and I was feeling optimistic.

Upon entering the doctor's office, tidbits of

apprehension entered my mind. The tumor was gone but what if it had been malignant? I refused to consider that possibility.

My doctor walked over to me and started to pull the staples out of my scalp. The whole thing was painless, and I envisioned myself stepping into the shower, feeling the pulsating rhythm of water beating upon my head, removing all the gook that had been underneath my bandage for ten days. The sweet smell of shampoo was on my mind.

My reverie was broken as soon as he spoke.

"Linda," he said in a lighthearted tone. "You have been the discussion of our tumor board this morning. The operation was successful, but unfortunately, the tumor was malignant. We now have to set up a protocol for you. I'll be sending you upstairs to oncology to receive all of the necessary information for your chemo regimen."

My stomach started to churn. I felt nauseous. Chemotherapy? I often swore that if I got cancer, I would never do chemotherapy. The stuff is poison. I saw what it had done to my father. Glancing over at Neil, I turned my head to the man who reminded me of Kris Kringle, and asked, "Am I going to die?"

"Oh my goodness, no! If you follow the regimen the oncologist prescribes, you could live another twenty years, as long as the tumor doesn't return. He has had tremendous success with the chemo and radiation clinical trials performed. I highly suggest you take this route."

"What about my seizures and the medication? Now that the tumor is gone, can I go off of the medicine?"

"I would advise you not to. The operation has caused

some scar tissue to form and that could trigger a seizure at any given time. I'm afraid you'll have to be on seizure medication the rest of your life."

"But I can drive now, right?"

"Not for another four months. You need to be seizure free for that period of time. We're finished for now. I've done my job, and now it's up to the oncologist to do his. You're going to be just fine. I hope I don't have to see you again."

And just like that, the person who saved my life dismissed me. Other lives were waiting for the skilled hands that would hopefully prevent their demise.

Neil intertwined his fingers with mine and led me out into the waiting room. For the third time in one month, Barbara and Moe joined us. They were waiting patiently to hear the news.

"Okay, let's go," Neil said as he looked at the two of them. I recognized the caution on his face. He didn't want to alarm them. "Linda's tumor was malignant, so now she has to see the oncologist upstairs. Supposedly, he's the best in this field. He will tell us what to do next."

Broad, fake smiles erupted on the faces of Moe and Barbara. They were alarmed but didn't reveal their concern.

Moe spoke first. "Well then, that is what we'll do. No need to worry. I'm sure he'll be able to allay any fears you have, Linda. All you need to do is follow his orders and you'll be fine."

Barbara kept quiet. I could just imagine how she felt. I was her only sibling, and both our parents were gone. Her fear must have been immense. Our differences in personalities never interfered with our love for each other. I knew in my heart, that if the roles had been reversed, I would be devastated at the thought of losing my sister. She knew I wasn't out of the woods yet.

Neil led the pack, as I trailed behind. Only one thought was on my mind. *What was the oncologist going to say? Would he prescribe chemo or radiation? Or was there no real solution?* My footsteps treaded heavily as we approached his office. I wanted to scream at Neil to make him realize how much I didn't want to be here but no sound escaped my lips as he opened the door.

The office waiting room was crowded. A sickening feeling came over me as I observed the dozens of people leaving. Wheelchairs, bruises from blood work, bald heads and pale faces were walking out the door. Yet as I watched closely, I saw the definite look of hope etched upon their face. Maybe that is what we all need. Hope; everlasting hope.

My name was called and Neil and I entered his office. The doctor's face was stern—not in an angry way—just a clinical way. Immediately I knew I was just another number to him. He had no jovial smile like the one my brain surgeon possessed. But who could blame him? He was here to do the dirty work after the surgeon succeeded. Suffering and death was probably a daily routine for him. I couldn't believe it. I actually had empathy for the man who was going to sentence me to the one thing I had dreaded all my life. Chemotherapy! I hadn't yet heard the word, but I knew it was coming. *What should I do?*

A long time ago, when my father was dying of pancreatic cancer, I witnessed the horrific side effects of the chemo drugs infused in his arm. He got violently sick, shook and was unable to function. His quality of life was diminished immensely. And still he died.

Then my mother fell ill eleven years later. She was diagnosed with colon cancer which metastasized to her liver. Six months was the time frame for her demise. We went together to the oncologist, and he suggested chemotherapy. Her fear ran deep and I saw her hesitate for a moment. She turned to me and asked me what she should do.

"I can't make that decision for you, Mom. But if you want to know what I would do, I can tell you. I wouldn't have chemo. I'll never forget what Dad went through."

We walked out of the office, never to return. Her decision was made. No chemotherapy. Six months later she was gone. Would she have survived if she'd had the chemo? I doubt it, but now here I stand with the same decision confronting me. Should I or shouldn't I, especially after I told her I would never do it. Would I be a hypocrite if I decided to allow them to put poison in my body?

I sat in the chair provided for me and glanced at this man who was to determine my fate. There was no empathy, just a matter-of-fact manner in his tone as the words spilled from his lips. "Linda, this is what you must do. Six months of chemo and two weeks of radiation. I think that will work. I realize you live far away, but we can set up this protocol in your area. But beware! When I tell these doctors your dose of chemo, they will be uncomfortable. We're going to be very aggressive with your dose, because I have found that it works. Many clinical trials have been performed with this type of tumor and we've had much success. Don't allow them to reduce your dose. I don't think you'll lose your hair, and with all of the anti-nausea drugs, you should be okay."

My oncologist paused for a moment and then continued to speak. "My only concern will be your blood counts. This chemo seems to attack the platelets. So they'll have to keep a close watch. You'll only have the dose once a month, because your body could not endure it more often. I think you'll be fine. When the chemo is finished, I'll expect to see you again to discuss the radiation. If all goes well, you have the chance to survive another twenty years. Good luck and we'll be in touch."

I was overwhelmed. Six months of chemo. I didn't even question it. Neil took my hand and squeezed it tight as I pondered my situation. This man who had betrayed me three years ago was now my rock. I could not imagine my life without him. We walked out of the office hand-in-hand and dealt the news to Barbara and Moe.

And so began the winter of my repose.

A PASSAGE THROUGH CHEMO
MY JOURNAL

I must digress here for a moment. I need to remind you that I'm no one exceptional. My life has been good, and like most people I know, it's been a comfortable one. Why this has happened to me is beyond my comprehension, but as you'll see, I'm not alone. Life can be unfair at times, but we all must learn the lessons we're taught. We might not know what they are at the time, but eventually they will be revealed to us. The journey I'm about to share with you demonstrates how courage, hope, love, faith and a deep appreciation for life helps us to sustain someone through difficult times.

Chemo Eve:

Ghosts and Goblins seem to surround me on this dark night. Tomorrow will be my first treatment, and it's Halloween, I sit and stare at the television, not even realizing what I'm watching. My mind is a million miles away. *Will I get sick? Will the poison help me?* Looking at Neil with tears in my eyes, I say goodnight. I pray that sleep will come quickly.

Day 1: Halloween

Rising out of bed in the morning after tossing and turning all night, I try to remain calm. While showering and delighting in the sweet smell of the soap, I try to convince myself that it won't be that bad. Who am I kidding? I'm willingly going to enter a room and allow them to put poison in my body. This can't be good.

I slip on a comfortable pair of jeans and my favorite sweatshirt. No use in getting dressed up for the occasion. Breakfast is out of the question. The butterflies are dancing in my stomach. An empty stomach will suffice.

I'm ready to go. The clinic is an hour away, so I have more time to fret. Staring at the road in front of the both of us, an unusual silence ensues. Normally we would chat and laugh about awful drivers, but nothing seems funny on this chilly, autumn day.

There it is, looming in the distance. The clinic I'd been to just last week for blood work. They said I was all set to go. Am I? Maybe physically, but not emotionally. I'm determined to don my mask of courage, in spite of the fear raging inside of me.

Dr. Price sits me down in his office. He explains the procedure. Sitting by my side, Neil listens to every word he says, but I am unable to concentrate. One pervasive thought keeps running through my mind. I want this over with.

The clinic is small and intimate. The nurse leads me to the room where I'll soon be hooked up to an IV dispensing the dreaded drug. There are recliners lined up against the wall, which actually appear inviting. Most of them are occupied, but one is waiting for me. I ease myself into the chair.

Clenched in my sweaty palms is my favorite magazine. *Do I really think I can concentrate on reading?* Soon the needle pokes my arm for the IV. Glancing around the room, I try to assess people's reactions to the chemo. Unlike me, they all seem undisturbed and very comfortable with what is happening. Me, I feel like I'm walking towards the platform for the guillotine. We're all fighting for our lives, but my acceptance is not forthcoming. I hope I can reach that point.

Questions run through my mind. *Will I be strong enough, or will I fail, like I have in so many aspects of my life?* Thoughts of my dear friend, Mary Ann, flood my mind. She's been fighting lung cancer for twelve years, but she never complains. I'm inspired by her courage.

Moving towards my chair, the nurse holds the drugs in her hand,

"Linda, first I'm going to administer a steroid to help with the nausea. It might make you feel a little edgy and your cheeks might flush. It also might make it difficult for you to sleep tonight. After the steroid I will be giving you an anti-nausea drug and then the chemo. The whole process will take at least an hour. I want you to let me know if you feel alright once we infuse the chemo."

"Okay," I say, with a slight edge in my voice. "Let's just get it over with."

The drip begins. I try desperately to concentrate on the crossword puzzle in front of me. Losing the fight, I stare at the clock, wishing I were somewhere else. My thoughts drift to my mother when she was dying. All alone in her struggle to survive, the anguish on her face was obvious. As much as I wanted to help her, I knew I couldn't. Her pain was her own, and trying to know what she felt was impossible. All I could do was be with her. It was a catch-22. She wanted me by her side, but she would get angry if I was there too often. When I would try to uplift her spirits, she'd become frustrated. But she knew she was leaving this world soon, and understood it was something you do alone. Standing in the shadow of her suffering, I began to understand the process of dying.

The minutes tick by slowly. My eyes dart towards the clock over and over again. Another patient talks to me. I start to relax. All of us speak about our cancer and what we need to do to survive. Everyone is optimistic and hope blossoms in this room like a newly planted garden. We're all flowers; some of us will die and some of us will live to see the next season.

The drip ends. After being unhooked from the IV, I say goodbye to my newly found comrades. I know I'll see them again.

Arriving home, we walk in the door and I'm welcomed with a beautiful bouquet of flowers. I tear open the card and realize it's from my lifelong friends, all of us members of the SCBG Club we formed while in college. My heart soars with the realization that my friends of thirty-two years have thought of me on one of the worst days of my life. Ever since the five of us left our crazy college days behind, we have remained very close.

Day 2:

Sleep is my enemy. The realm of deep unconsciousness was nowhere to be found
last night. The steroids had taken effect. I tossed and turned all night.

As soon as I rise out of bed, I down the anti-nausea pills even though I don't feel sick. I'm feeling slightly elated by the fact I'm not throwing up. In fact, I seem to have a surplus of energy, although I haven't slept well. I suppose the steroids have helped. Maybe chemo won't be so bad.

Day 3:

I slept better last night. There were no dreams. I awake easily and take the pills once again. The nurse told me to take them for at least three days, even though they gave me the anti-nausea medicine in my IV. I'm not going to screw around with those orders.

Neil is already awake and tending to Kevin. Skipping down the stairs, anxious to see my husband and darling angel Kevin, I feel my first wave of nausea. Pushing it back, I hope it won't resurface. But it does with a vengeance. Our bathroom becomes my private haven. Just like my mother, suffering has taken its toll.

Day 4:

The poison courses through my veins. I'm very sick. It's worse than yesterday. The nausea is overpowering. Every step to the bathroom is exhausting. My mind is clouded with illness. There will be no more writing today.

Day 5:

The sun rises brightly and I'm feeling a little better. The nausea is subsiding and food is looking good. The neglected housework summons me. Laundry, dishes and vacuuming seems like a treat. After accomplishing these tasks, a three-hour nap ensues. I want to feel normal, but can't seem to find that place. My hands shake as I realize normal is a thing of the past. My world has been turned upside down. I'm sick. Even Neil's affair seems trivial.

Day 6:

A tiny wave of nausea appears from nowhere. My pills are done. Eating might make me feel better. Maybe I can do this. If this is all that happens, then dealing with it will be easy. If only the fatigue was less. That is the most difficult part. Resting is imperative. I just want to get better.

Day 7:

Upon awakening this morning, there is no stomach upset. I delight in the lack of queasiness. Three more weeks before this cycle begins again. I refuse to think about it. One day at a time. Once again the fatigue is overwhelming. Every task seems insurmountable. Please don't ask me to do anything.

Neil has been wonderful. If it wasn't for him, I'm not sure I could endure this.

Day 8:

Life has returned to normal. I'm not sure what that means, but I'm now resuming my responsibilities that have been forsaken for a whole week. Feeling great wouldn't actually describe my state of being, but at least I'm able to function. A long nap is necessary every day. I glance around my home and wish I could accomplish the tasks I used to do with joy. The laundry piles up, shopping is a thing of the past, and the couch constantly beckons me. I'm succumbing to the trials and tribulations of chemo. This too will pass (I hope).

Day 33:

Many days have passed. Resuming my usual routine is a welcome diversion to the impending second treatment soon on the horizon. I was supposed to receive chemo the day after Thanksgiving, but it's been postponed until Monday. Cancer can wait for the holiday. A few days don't seem to matter.

My sister and her husband joined us for the feast of turkey, stuffing, cranberry sauce and apple pie. I was so happy to have them here. My brain tumor took a backseat. For the first time in a month, a nap wasn't necessary. Monday seemed to be eons away as I took pleasure having my family with me.

Tomorrow is my next treatment. Today is Sunday and Neil is at work. My sister returned home. I'm left alone with Kevin and my thoughts. He and I play, but my heart isn't in it. More often than not, I love to sit and watch him play. Every little accomplishment is a huge milestone. It's thrilling to watch him press the buttons necessary to play music on his keyboard. The simplest of tasks are like a miracle to me, especially when I see the delight on his face. But today I can't seem to concentrate. Tomorrow looms on the horizon. Anxiety sets in and I walk away from Kevin, lost in my own scary notions of what I'll feel like these next few days. Will this treatment be as easy as the last one, or does it get worse? I can only wait and see.

Gazing out the window, I watch the leaves cascade to the ground. Winter is coming. The days are short, enveloping us in the cloak of darkness so as to match my mood. I lay Kevin down for the night. My quiet time is filled with dread about tomorrow.

Day 34:

As I roll over in bed, the cool autumn sun shines in my eyes. Awareness of the day and what it means reaches my level of consciousness. Wiping the sleep from my eyes, my heart flutters. I rise out of bed and welcome Kevin to a brand new day. His giggles and laughter help to allay my fears. The bus picks him up for day treatment, where I know he will be happy.

As the water beats steadily upon my scar, I wonder if I'll lose my hair. Dr. Gruber at NYU said I probably won't, but almost everyone in the clinic receiving chemo is bald. Will I be the exception?

Our arrival is timely, but because of the holiday, I'm at a different clinic farther away. It's located near my girlfriend's home. We have made a tentative lunch date depending on how I feel. If this one is similar to the first one, I know I'll be fine.

The infusion lasts an hour, same as before, and I'm less tense. I'm able to finish the crossword puzzle this time. Neil arrives just as I am finished and he asks me how I feel.

"Fine," I reply. "Let's call Patti and tell her we'll be at the restaurant shortly." His
relief is evident. I'm ravenous. The steroids seem to have that effect on me. Seeing Patti lifts my spirits. We have been friends for years, since our days at college. Talking to her makes me feel better. Soon after lunch, I'm ready to go home.

Once again as we enter our house, another beautiful floral arrangement is sitting on the table. I knew it was from our SCBG group. Patti never mentioned it. I can feel my friends here with me. Expressing my gratitude, will take years, and I hope God grants me that time.

Day 35:

I expected I wouldn't sleep well last night, and I didn't.

The mega-dose of steroids kept me fitful for hours. Extreme fatigue is upon me once more. My stomach keeps cramping up, but I can deal with that. Food is not appealing right now. I'm craving the deep, dark slumber for an escape.

Day 36:

This morning I feel very well rested. I'm taking my pills and don't seem to be sick to my stomach. Unfortunately, I'm constipated. This drug doesn't seem to be able to make up its mind. Water has become the drink of choice to help flush the chemo out of my body. I've loved drinking water, but at this moment I detest it. Running to the bathroom every few minutes is exhausting. They say the drug will remain in my system for quite some time. Being hydrated is important. Chemotherapy happens to be cumulative, so I'm told.

The more you get the worse it gets. I hope they are wrong.

Today isn't that bad. Maybe I'm able to bear this regimen.

Day 37:

Am I crazy? I'm so sick I can't even describe it. Maybe I'll write tomorrow.

Day 38:

This isn't funny anymore. I'll talk to you when the world seems brighter and lighter than it is today.

Day 39:

Unable to get off the couch, I catch a glimpse of the

bathroom, which seems miles away. I don't like what is happening to my body. Why have I allowed them to poison me?

Day 40:

The sickness is subsiding, yet fatigue overwhelms me. This lumpy, uncomfortable couch has become my best friend. Television seems to be the only distraction for now. I dream of the day I'll be up and running around again.

Day 41:

Feeling better, I shower, running my fingers through wet, squeaky-clean hair. My hand massages the scar, which feels like a series of lumps across the back of my head. I no longer feel squeamish when I remember that awful day. A craniotomy was a picnic compared to chemo.

Day 42:

I'm feeling better, but I can't seem to shake the fatigue. How will I ever manage Christmas? The thought of shopping, Christmas cards, decorating, and entertaining is filling me with anxiety.

Day 55:

The snow is falling like angels in flight and leaves its soft, white blanket upon the ground. Today is Christmas. The dread and anxiety of the holiday has left my soul. With the help of Neil, our house is decorated and I find pleasure watching the twinkling white lights of the

Christmas tree dance in the window. There is a true peace within me, along with a resurgence of hope.

Unfortunately, my little angel, Kevin has not been feeling well. A trip to the doctor and prescribed medicines does not seem to be helping. A good portion of the day is spent consoling him while I try to entertain our guests for the holiday. Thankfully, we're a small group this year. Only my son Eric and Jim, our long time resident at the Inn, are present at the table with us. This seems to be fitting for a Christmas before my next treatment. Peace and quiet is welcome.

Day 56:

I'm having trouble with my seizure medicine. My body is covered with an angry rash. With haste, Neil calls the neurologist and a new drug is prescribed. Hopefully the rash will go away. The incessant itching is becoming a nuisance. I suppose this is the least of my worries.

On another note, Kevin is very sick. Last night he kept us awake all night, throwing up. He doesn't understand what is happening and my heart goes out to him. His doctor told us to bring him to the emergency room for a stomach x-ray and some blood work. These episodes of sickness occur too often. Kevin's disability makes it difficult for doctors to diagnose what is wrong and causes a tremendous amount of anxiety for us.

Wheeling Kevin into the emergency room, we're aware there will be a long wait. Kevin isn't happy and neither am I. Like most people I want him to be tended to right away. Neil paces the floor and I hold Kevin in my arms. For now, my cancer seems like a distant memory. My main concern is Kevin.

The waiting room is crowded and the sun shines brightly in our eyes through the massive window. An angel appears disguised as a lovely woman. She sits across the room from us and stares at Kevin, not with a look of repugnance, but with a sincere expression of empathy. Reaching out to me, she asks if we would like to sit beside her to alleviate the sun from beating in our eyes. I lift Kevin and we sit beside this lovely woman. At first no words are spoken. The sun continues to beat upon my back as I glance sideways towards her. I witness her hesitation as she asks the question I knew would be forthcoming.

"What is wrong with him?"

Being familiar with this inquiry, I have no problem answering. "He's microcephalic
and severely disabled. We're here because he's ill and will probably become dehydrated if we can't get him to drink. We're waiting to have some x-rays done. But I'm becoming impatient and Kevin is starting to get distressed."

Her empathy is evident. She pauses for a moment. "I'm sorry I was staring, but I have a severely disabled son also. He has a rare degenerative brain disease that has become increasingly difficult for him. He can't walk, talk, swallow or function in any way that is familiar to us. But his smile is as genuine as the smile I see upon your son's face. He emanates love, and as I watch you, I know you feel the same way I do. He is a gift, isn't he?"

"Yes, he is. But it breaks my heart when I watch him suffer."

"I know what you mean. Three times the doctors have told me to prepare for my son's funeral, and each time he has defeated the odds. I have grown to love his smiling face and tidbits of laughter." Her smile disappears. A few years ago I lost my teenage son in a fight at a party he had gone to. An argument erupted and my son was stabbed to death. I was devastated, and I don't think I can handle another loss."

I listen and become aware of the courage and determination she possesses. She never raises her voice and isn't looking for pity. She is accepting of her lot in life and willing to make the best of it. I had to ask. "Why are you here right now?"

"I have some sort of stomach problem, and they can't seem to diagnose what's wrong. I just want to get better so I can go home and be with my son. He needs me."

All of my problems seemed to float away. How could I be so blind to other people's
misfortunes?

I look at the clock, feeling Kevin squirming in my arms. I realize I need to leave. We can't wait any longer. I say goodbye to the woman who has touched my soul, and I take my baby home. I'll nurse him back to health by myself. As we enter our home, I see a twinkle in Kevin's eyes and right away he starts to drink. His distress is gone. I sit and reflect on my meeting with this woman whose name I never asked. Her face remains etched in my mind. I believe I encountered an angel while sitting in the emergency room as the sun sparkled in our eyes.

Day 57:

Kevin seems to be fine. He is drinking, eating and playing as usual. In my heart I believe God has sent me an answer to my prayers.

I begin my new seizure medicine. I can't seem to catch my breath these past few days. Is the seizure med or chemo causing this new condition? After walking up our few stairs, I feel compelled to sit down. I feel like I can't breathe. It's exhausting me.

The phone rings, its tone piercing. My friend is on the line checking up on me. She was an oncology nurse for ten years and wants to know how I feel. I tell her I'm having trouble breathing. As long as I sit still I'm fine, but any exertion has me totally winded. She is concerned.

"Linda, you must tell your oncologist. This can be a serious side effect from the
chemo. Don't fool around. Talk to him."

"I will. I promise. My next chemo is New Year's Eve, and I'll see him then. So far they say my blood work is fine. I'll wait and see."

We say goodbye, but not after I promise I will keep her abreast of what is happening.

Day 58:

My rash is horrific. The itching doesn't cease. No one seems to know what is causing it. I personally think it is the chemo. Cortisone creams aren't helping. I'll just have to tolerate the red blistering bumps all over my legs, stomach and back. I can't decide which is worse; the incessant itching or not being able to breathe.

Day 59:

Today I get my blood work done in preparation for the third dose of chemo. I'm beginning to frustrate the nurses. Their frustration mounts as they have trouble tapping my veins. They suggest a port be put in my chest, but I adamantly refuse. I can't handle another invasive procedure. I don't relish being difficult, but this is my body and I have the right to refuse certain things. I'm becoming a fast learner. I used to think you had to do everything the doctors and nurses told you, but now I realize I can stand my ground on certain issues. A port in my chest is one of them.

Day 60:

Today is uneventful. I try desperately not to think about tomorrow. Worrying is a
waste my precious time. I can never have these moments back. When will I learn?

Day 61:

It's New Year's Eve, and for most people, a day of celebration, champagne, hats, horns, music and dancing. There will be no rejoicing for me. I find no reason to celebrate. Chemo will be coursing through my body on this day. Knowing what is in store for me leaves my body heavy with dread. I will sit home alone tonight feeling sorry for myself. There are no resolutions this year, just the hope that I will survive.

Day 62:

The flowers were on the table again when I returned home, but this time there were two arrangements. Someone must have screwed up and sent flowers when it wasn't their turn. The laughter felt good. My crazy friends. I love them more than they will ever realize.

The New Year has begun. My chemo treatment went fine. Similar to the other two, today I'm okay. My sleep was interrupted last night because of the steroids, but I knew what to expect. I suppose it's the lesser of two evils.

No sleep or vomiting. I choose the lack of sleep. After laying Kevin down for a nap, I decide to rest my head upon the pillow.

I awake with a start as I hear Kevin's caregiver enter his room. Releasing the fog that surrounds my head is difficult, but I manage a weak smile. We don't even talk and soon my eyes are closing allowing me to enter the world of dreams where sickness lay far behind.

Day 63:

Violently sick. Is it the flu? My body aches, nausea overwhelms me, and every movement is a tremendous effort. Where is the bathroom?

Day 64:

Today is worse than yesterday. I can't move my bowels and the nausea is horrible. I sit upon the cold floor of the bathroom resting my head on the toilet. Nothing comes up, but I am too weak to get up. I lay there for quite some time, praying this will end.

Neil stops home to check on me and by this time I am back on the couch with no recollection of how I got there. I don't acknowledge his presence. I want to be alone in my misery.

Day 65:

I'm able to drink some water today and sit upright in the chair. The nausea still creeps in and I try to ignore the sick feeling in my stomach. As long as I sit still, I'm fine. Well, fine is a relative term. I guess I feel better than yesterday. Frustration has become an everyday occurrence. I want to do things, but whenever I try to accomplish the simplest of tasks, I find myself collapsing in the chair. Trying to go upstairs is like I'm climbing Mt. Everest.

I have a great deal of time to think. My mother comes to mind. I witnessed her dying and am now starting to understand what it's like.

Day 66:

Kevin was sick last night. His caregiver has the day off so I tend to Kevin's needs all by myself. Since he isn't feeling well this task is simple. We both lie on the couch and watch television. Hopefully tomorrow will be better.

Day 67:

Kevin is much better today and has gone to his day treatment program. I wish I could say the same for me. Depression has set in and Neil's sordid affair creeps back into my thoughts. As I sit here and ponder the events leading up to his indiscretion, I fight back waves of nausea. My fixation on his affair will have to wait for another day; I'm too tired to give a crap.

Day 68:

For the first time in days I am able to take a shower. Drying off, I sit on the floor to catch my breath and the tears begin again. I'm not sure why I'm crying, but the release feels good. My hair, which I still possess, smells of fresh lavender, and the clothes I put on have the sweet fragrance of fabric softener. I wish I could feel as fine as this pleasant aroma. Assuring myself this will happen, I wipe away the tears.

Day 69:

The sun shines brilliantly outside. My mind begins to wander. Looking out, I imagine myself relaxing on a chaise lounge, luxuriating in the warmth of the sun. I step outside and the reverie is over. It's freezing outside. Winter is here with all of its fury.

Lying on the couch will have to suffice.

Today holds the promise of taking a ride in the car. You would think it odd to be excited about such a trivial thing. It's amazing how appreciation for the little things in life awakens when you are ill. We should all remember this.

Day 70:

Another brilliant, sunny day, but I'm not fooled. The temperature outside is twenty degrees below zero. Kevin is home because of the cold. Today is my appointment with my neurologist. I call Kevin's caregiver. She isn't happy to be awakened so early. My concern for her is minimal.

My neurologist is so cute. Every time I see him he apologizes for taking me off the seizure medication after my first episode. I assure him he probably saved my life. If the second seizure hadn't occurred, the tumor might not have been found until it was too late.

But I wasn't seeing him for that. My oncologist prescribed xanax for me to help reduce my anxiety. I want to know if I can take it safely with my seizure medication. My neurologist assures me it will be fine.

Day 71:

Life goes on as usual. I sleep quite a bit, but maybe that is my body's way of repairing itself. Kevin is home once again, and we enjoy our day together.

Day 88:
Many days have passed. I feel better, but the fatigue and shortness of breath is ever-present. Neil took me to Atlantic City with our good friends, Sal and Marietta. We had a wonderful time. Being by the ocean renewed my spirit.

I had my blood work done last week. The fourth treatment is in two days. I keep praying to God He will allow this to end. My dear friend who is an oncology nurse, tells me the doctors never stop chemo treatments until they are finished. This information does not deter my prayers. There are always exceptions to the rule.

Day 89:
Tis the night before chemo. Sitting here all alone wrapped in my cloak of fear and trepidation, my prayers are constant. Please make this end. The sickness is worse each time. Complaining doesn't help, but I'm scared. How much can my body take? Neil isn't home tonight, so I'm left alone with my fears. The thought of opening the door to the clinic brings on waves of nausea. I'm dreading tomorrow. Please, God, help me.

Day 90:
I manage to walk through the door. The xanax has helped, but my hands are shaking. This is my fourth treatment, and instead of feeling better, I'm feeling worse. This place gives me the creeps.

Dr. Price calls me into his office. A reprieve from chemo is given. The blood work has shown a tremendous drop in my red and white blood cell count. This seems to be the reason for the shortness of breath. I'm horribly anemic and have no immune system.

Chemo is out of the question. He tells me to return on Monday to receive more blood work. This will determine whether or not the chemo can continue. Before leaving, I'm given a shot of Aranesp to restore my red blood cells. Hopefully, breathing will be easier.

Elation is the first emotion, but dismay quickly follows. I'm putting off the inevitable. Chemo will win.

Day 93:

A few days have passed, and I have not written a word in my journal. My head feels like it will explode and I can't seem to clear the cobwebs in my brain. Standing up brings on a dizziness that is overwhelming. Kevin's caregiver needs to be here. I call her and she arrives immediately. I lie down and my brain succumbs to the unconscious state of mind it so desires.

Tonight is Super Bowl Sunday. The party will go on without me. I miss the fun and camaraderie of the days when being healthy was taken for granted.

Day 94:

My thoughts are clearer today. Last night was unpleasant. Kevin was sick again, but once his episode was over, he seemed to be fine. Hopefully my immune system will keep me from catching whatever virus he had. While keeping my distance from him, his caregiver tends to his needs. We sit in separate rooms and his hugs are given to someone else.

Day 95:

The phone rang this morning and a dear friend of mine was on the other end. I'm awash in my emotion about the impending chemo, so idle chit chat isn't on my mind. Hearing her voice makes me realize I want to talk to her. She is my chemo aficionado. Her reassurance is helpful.

I place the phone back on its receiver, gaze outside and watch the snowflakes cascading to the ground. Happy to be inside, Kevin sits and hugs me as we listen to the melodic music of Yanni. My rash is acting up again. Neil will arrive home soon, and I can feel the relief from the itch already. He will scratch my legs and rub ointment on them, like he does every night. This is the highlight of my day.

Kevin goes to bed and my apprehension about tomorrow returns. My prayers are endless. God, please put a stop to this. I realize my friend Kathy has told me that won't happen, but I am filled with hope. Maybe a miracle is on the horizon.

Day 96:

The snow is beautiful, but not enough to interfere with us driving to the clinic. Our arrival is timely. My heart palpitates as the door opens. *Am I allowed to scream?* Someone must recognize my fear. Someone. Anyone. But there is no hint that anybody does. Even Neil, as he grips my hand tightly, has no idea concerning the terror deep inside of me.

We're leaving. No chemo today. Now my platelets have plummeted and if my bloodwork shows no improvement by next week, I might need a blood transfusion. I erase my thoughts. The shot of Aranesp was administered and we're on our way to Saratoga. It's been six weeks since my last chemo and I' feeling pretty good. I might as well enjoy this day. Shopping and dinner at the track is fun. The trotters are running tonight and the races are entertaining.

Day 100:

A longtime friend and resident at our Inn is very ill. For twenty years he's been an interesting part of our lives. At eighty-six years old, Jim has never married and is an only child. He is smart, observant and quite a character. For many years he graced us with his presence at thanksgiving and Christmas. Always nattily dressed in a suit, tie and fedora—the finest brooks brothers would have—he's fully decked out even in 90 degree weather.

He's unique; one of a kind. The Jim stories are numerous and we're sad to be witnessing his decline. He doesn't seem to know where he is and spends most of the day in bed. Neil is worried. We must take Jim to the doctor, but Neil hesitates. Jim has been to the doctor once in his life and swore he would never go again. I understand Neil's reluctance to go against Jim's wishes, but soon it will be necessary.

Day 101:

More blood work today. The needle is having trouble finding my veins. The nurse continues to poke around. Turning my head away, I withstand the deep ache within my arm. She tells me she is done. This will determine whether or not I'll receive my chemo in two days. I dread the sickness that will ensue, but I'm resigned to the fact it must be done. This horrible invader must be conquered.

My prayers for this to end have not been answered, but I'm not angry. Why should God grant me divine intervention? I'm no one special. Many other people have suffered more greatly than I.

Day 102:

Tomorrow is supposed to be my next dose. I feel wonderful today. My energy level is high and my breathing comes easily. The house is clean again and I find myself contemplating cooking a meal. Nothing too ambitious, but something I know Neil enjoys. Hamburger Helper, salad and garlic bread are on the menu for tonight. He will be pleased.

Day 103:

Chemo is a go. My blood counts rose enough to receive the fourth dose. I know what to expect. It could be worse this time, but I'm ready for whatever happens. No matter what it takes, this army of strangers inside my brain will be defeated. They will not win.

As I sit in the recliner, watching the drip slowly enter my body, my mind wanders. Why am I gaining weight? People with cancer usually lose excess pounds. I imagine being born during the Renaissance. Somewhere there would be a portrait of me hanging on a wall, portraying a very full bodied figure. A quiet chuckle escapes my mouth as these thoughts course through my mind. The reverie is broken as the nurse unhooks my drip. I'm finished for the day.

The nurse informs me that Dr. Price wants to speak with me. I can't imagine why. I sit with Neil in the waiting room and soon I am called into the doctor's office.

"Linda, sit down. This is your fourth treatment and we feel it would be a good idea for you to return to NYU to see your other oncologist again. You should make an appointment soon before we schedule you for the fifth treatment. Take your MRI w-rays with you. The dose of carboplatin you are receiving is very high and is attacking your good cells. I would like his opinion before we continue."

Neil and I leave the office and turn to each other without saying a word. What could we possibly talk about? Another hurdle to overcome? We're both tired.

Day 104:

Millions of crazy thoughts run through my mind. When I go to NYU, will he say I am finished?Will Or will he at least reduce the last dose? I have to wait and see.

As usual, I'm feeling fine today. Of course, "fine" is a relative term. I'm not sick yet. But this seems to be the protocol.

Today is my son Kyle's birthday and anniversary. He's been married one year today. I call to wish him a happy birthday, as I enter the clinic once again. I was just there yesterday, but need to be back again today. The doctor insists that I receive these shots to help bring up my blood cell counts. I am so sick of all of this. I desperately want it to end.

My hand shakes as I turn the knob to the door. I don't want to be here. They administer my shot of Neulasta to bring up my white blood cell count. As I rise to leave, the nurse orders me to sit down.

"Linda, we want you to wait about twenty minutes. Sometimes people have a reaction to this shot, and we want to make sure that you are okay. Just relax for awhile."

I do as I'm told and silently pray to God. *"Please let my oncologist at NYU tell me I'm done with this. I need your help. My strength is waning."*

Day 105:

Today is Friday the 13th. A very fitting day for how I feel. Nausea, dizziness, and the overwhelming urge to sleep. I'm miserable. Please let this day end.

Day 106:

Today is Valentine's Day. Who cares? Kyle and Jenny stopped by, but left in a hurry when they recognized my distress. My social graces are gone.

Day 107:

The sickness persists. I lift my head to look out the window and become aware of the sunshine. The sky is so blue, but soon my head is back upon the pillow and I cry tears of anguish, frustration, but most of all fear. I don't want to die, but during this single moment, death seems to be welcoming me.

Day 108:

Am I repeating myself? I feel horrible. I can't eat and drinking water is such an effort. How long will this last? Can I really survive two more treatments?

Spring is right around the corner. The shadows cast by the sun are longer than they were. I need to feel the rebirth that spring can bring.

Day 109:

The pulse of the shower feels wonderful. It's been five days since my tired, aching body has been able to climb our stairs. The energy is drained out of my body. I luxuriate in the feeling of cleanliness and toss my rank pajamas into the hamper. They will be washed later. Right now, I need to sit down.

Kevin is home today because of the holiday. His caregiver has the day off. The phone interrupts our playtime, and my friend Mary offers to come over. I welcome her suggestion to help me with Kevin. The thoughtfulness of this act overwhelms me, and I sit down and cry. Way too often my tears flow freely, and I am embarrassed by my own emotions.

The knock on the door is barely audible. The weakness in my legs makes me stumble as I go to the door. Mary enters and tells me to sit down. She plays with Kevin as I put my feet up to relax. She feeds him, changes him and he lies down for a good night's sleep. I'm so thankful for her help, but at a loss for words. Mary says goodbye and tells me to call her whenever I need to. Flopping on the couch, I await Neil's arrival. Maybe I'll be able to eat tonight.

Day 110:

Dinner tasted good last night, but didn't hang around for long. The bathroom called my name all night.

I don't feel like going to Johnstown for more blood work. My arm is beginning to feel like a pincushion. Hopefully the results will be good.

Going out to lunch isn't on the agenda. I need my couch. We returned home and the phone is ringing as I open the door. Our friend Jim is getting worse and Neil leaves in haste. I'm too tired to care. Sleep descends upon me immediately.

There is an incessant ringing. It must be the phone. I pick up the receiver while the confusion that sleep induces leaves me unsure of where I am. My sister is on the other end and is sobbing hysterically.

"Barbara, what's wrong?" I ask while trying to clear the cobwebs from my mind.

"My house burnt down last night. Rob and I are fine, but we lost everything. I was at work and Rob had a fire going in the woodstove. He was watching TV, and all of a sudden he saw flames climbing up the wall. The fire department came, but in order to put the fire out, they had to tear down the walls. The only thing left is the shell of the house and our kitchen. Thankfully they saved our photo albums. I don't even have a toothbrush or toothpaste. I don' know where to begin. I wish you could be here with me."

I started to cry, not only for my sister's pain but also for mine.

"Oh my God! I wish I could be with you, but I can't. I'm too sick to go anywhere. I'm so sorry. Why do things go wrong at inappropriate times? If I was better I would be there now. This must be a nightmare for you."

Our crying abated and we both commiserated about our lives. I'm sick and she has lost her home. Life can seem so unfair at times.

Day 111:

Neil has made my appointment with the oncologist at NYU. We'll be returning there in two weeks. I foolishly keep praying that he will end the chemo, but I know better. At the very least I hope he will tell me the drug is working.

I'm still not feeling well and have started to believe my days of feeling well are gone forever. Jim has become a huge concern for us. He doesn't seem to recognize anyone and lies in bed all day. Neil calls me. "Linda, I need to take Jim to the doctor. Can you possibly come with me?"

"Of course, "I reply, but my heart isn't in it. I think about the situation and realize Neil needs me now, more for moral support than anything else. How can I possibly let him down, after all he has done for me?

I'm dressed and waiting as Neil pulls in the driveway with a less- than-cogent Jim. My knees buckle as I step out the door, but I catch myself and hide my weakness. At this moment, Neil needs me to be strong.

We arrive at the doctor, and right away Jim is admitted to the hospital. As Neil wheels Jim down the long corridor, I'm fifty feet behind. I can't keep up. I tell him to go ahead and I'll be there shortly. We enter the CT scan room and the tests begin. I sit in the chair, catching my breath while fighting off waves of nausea. How could all this be happening? The answers don't come.

Day 112:

We're going to see Jim today and hopefully they will have some results. I realize he is eighty-six-years old, but he has never been sick a day in his life. It's difficult to watch someone you care about deteriorate so quickly.

The doctor meets us in his room. Jim will not be coming home. He has lung cancer, which has metastasized to the brain. The consensus is he has about two weeks to live.

Neil has a dentist appointment, and I tell him to go. Moving slowly, I sit beside Jim and watch him sleep.

Why is it so difficult for the soul to leave the body? I witnessed this battle when my mother was dying. I can see it's time for Jim to let go, yet his body clings to life. Why do we fight the inevitable? Maybe the thought of no more sunsets, no more waves beating upon the shore, no more laughter, no more blue skies makes us hang on to something that is already gone. I don't know, but I'm aware the process of dying is slow, when you sit and witness it. There should be a better way. Hasn't euthanasia remained a controversial issue?

Neil returns from the dentist. We say goodbye to Jimmy, telling him we'll be back tomorrow.

Day 113:

We're back to see Jim. Nothing has changed. The morphine drips slowly into his IV and I find comfort in the fact that he isn't in pain. Drowsiness comes over me as I sit beside Jim. My nausea has subsided, but food is not appealing to me. My numerous bottles of water will hopefully help to keep flushing the chemo out of my body. As I sit and daydream, I envision myself sitting at NYU with my oncologist as he tells me my chemo is over. Jim stirs and my reverie is broken. Reality sets in. There are two more treatments to deal with.

Day 114:

I'm filled with a depression, unlike any I have ever encountered. There is no reason to feel this way. Nothing bad has happened, yet my tears are incessant and I can't wipe them away fast enough. Feeling sorry for myself is abhorrent to me. Then the memory comes flooding back. Today is the anniversary of my mother's death. Maybe being with Jim is making me recall haunting memories.

Day 120:

A few days have gone by with nothing new to report. Jim is getting worse, and we continue to see him every day.

My prayers never stop. I want this chemo regimen to end. I relay these thoughts to my friends, and once again I am gently reminded to be strong and stop wishing for the impossible. I tell them to go to hell. How can they possibly understand what I'm going through? It's not their fault. I would be the same way. We all imagine ourselves as being truly empathetic, but the truth is; no one can ever fully comprehend someone else's anguish. Deep in my heart, I realize they are trying their best to comfort me, but they can still go to hell!

Day 121:

It sure is cold outside, but the sun beating through my window causes my eyes to shut. The dreams begin and I retreat to my favorite place where the air is warm and the palm trees sway. I love being there, even if it is only a dream. Something disturbs my sleep. I think it was ice falling off the roof. The warm air and palm trees are gone. The snow is covering the ground and I wonder if summer will ever arrive.

I remain steadfast in my determination to beat this overpowering depression. In my mind nothing seems to be going right. Jim is dying and I still have two more treatments. It's hard to appreciate being alive when you feel so poorly. I remind myself that every day is a gift and I should not waste even one.

I'm alone with my thoughts. Kevin is at program, Neil is out of town running errands, and Kyle and Eric are working. I consider my appointment at NYU. Many questions enter my mind. I write them down. The list is long. Are my MRI's okay? Can I dye my hair? (It desperately needs it). Are my blood counts interfering with the chemo regimen? When can I drive again? Will I have to be on seizure medication the rest of my life? How long after the chemo will radiation begin? Will they shave my head for radiation? What will be the side effects? Is my prognosis good? Did chemo cause this horrific rash I have?

I glance at the list and an unusual fear crawls up my spine. Am I going to survive? Why have I not been afraid of dying before?

Day 122:

More blood work. My body is a pincushion and my veins are tired. The nurses are frustrated with my veins. I don't even care anymore. Maybe the doctor will end all of this.

Tomorrow is my MRI. I'd rather have spiders crawling all over me than have to enter that claustrophobic cylinder again. They didn't bother me in the beginning, but after having so many of them, I have come to despise the whole procedure. Sleep will not come easy tonight as I lie awake in anticipation of this test.

Day 123:

As I rise out of bed, my anxiety level is heightened. I dress quickly as Neil puts Kevin on the bus. While fixing a cup of tea, I pop a xanax. This should keep me calm.

Holding hands, Neil and I walk down the corridor to enter the mobile van where the MRI will take place. For some reason, I feel relaxed. The xanax is doing its job. The technicians are kind and lead me to the bed I will lie on. Headphones with music are placed over my ears as I don my night blinders. Wearing these helps to keep my eyes closed. This way I don't realize how closed in I am. The panic button is in my right hand, and the stretcher is wheeled inside the machine. The technician speaks softly and tells me to lay perfectly still. I certainly have heard those instructions before. I feel a twinge in my neck as I try not to move. The thunderous hammering sound begins. Without the headphones the noise would be deafening. The vibrations from the machine help to soothe me. A voice tells me I'm being pulled out of this claustrophobic contraption, but I still must remain motionless. The technician calls for a phlebotomist and she arrives in a timely manner. My neck aches. I want to turn my head, but I can't. Some sort of mask has my head bolted to the table. As I lie still, she sticks the needle in my arm. A warm sensation courses through my body; I taste the dye in my mouth and soon smell it in my nostrils. The stretcher is wheeled back in. I try not to panic and convince myself to remain calm. The hammering begins once again and my toes wiggle to the beat of each noise. Each second seems like an eternity, but soon the stretcher is wheeled out of the machine. It's over. Relief washes over my tense body. Now I just have to wait to see what the results are. This MRI could be my defining moment. Only my oncologist can decide.

Day 124:

The icicles drip as the sun's rays beat down upon them. They look like huge crystals glittering outside the window. March has arrived and more snow is on the way. Winter's fury isn't ending soon. This is a winter I'll never forget. I spend a great deal of time staring outside as life passes me by. I hope to be able to rejoin the human race someday. Am I feeling sorry for myself? You bet I am.

I'm finished doing payroll for the Inn and think about what today will bring. We're going to see Jim again. I'm hoping he is better.

We enter Jim's room. Immediately I notice his condition is worsening. He doesn't acknowledge our presence. This situation is difficult for Neil as he considers Jim to be like
a father to him. We both sit quietly and watch the rise and fall of Jim's chest as he breathes slowly. There is nothing to talk about. He is dying, and we don't know what to say to each other. We silently pray.

I sit by Jim's side and whisper, "It's okay, Jim. Don't be afraid. Your mother is waiting for you."

I get no reply. Neil paces back and forth and jingles the keys in his pocket. He struggles with his emotions. "Come on Neil." I say. "It's time for us to leave. We'll be back again tomorrow."

Day 125:

We arrived at the hospital. I picked up my MRI and all of the paperwork for my visit to the establishment I so highly feared at the beginning of this ordeal. Four more days and I will be in NYC again.

The hospice nurse is by Jim's side when we enter the room. She informs us that it won't be much longer. There is an air of sadness amongst us but none of us are surprised. Neil and I sit with Jim for quite some time; both of us entrenched in our memories of days gone by.

I realize the impact he has had on my life. I wish I had appreciated him more.

Day 126:

Fatigue jolts me like a bolt of lightning. My head aches, my neck aches, even my toes ache. Sometimes I used to go to work with serious hangovers, and I felt better then than I do now. This is what chemo does to you. I'm hoping if anyone reads this, he or she will better understand what people endure when they undertake this course of therapy. I understand everyone has his or her own experience, but many thought and feelings, physical or mental, will be similar to mine. I have kept this journal, not only for myself, but also for the people going through the same thing, and even for the people facing the prospect of cancer treatment. There are millions of us out there. We need to know we are not alone.

I'm home today. No long treks to the hospital, no blood work, and no tests. Just a day to relax my weary body, and lie around with Kevin. Tomorrow we'll leave for New York City. For some odd reason, I'm excited about going and don't understand why.

Day 127:

Neil is at work and Kevin plays with his toys. My bags are packed. We'll be leaving around 11am. My elation is persistent. I don't question the feeling.

Our first stop is the hospital to see Jim. We hate to leave him, but this trip is necessary. Upon entering Jim's room we could see he wasn't doing well. His breathing is labored and I recognize the death rattle I heard when my mother was dying.

Neil seems nervous and agitated. He leaves the room to confer with the nurses. I slide my chair over to Jim to be by his side. Whispering in his ear, I tell him it's time. He needs to leave this world and be at peace. But before I finish speaking, I grasp his old worn out hand and ask a favor.

"Jim, I know the time is near and you are going to the place we'll all be one day. I 'm certain you'll be happy. But could you promise me something? When you arrive, would you please ask God to end my horrible chemo? I realize this is a lot to ask, but maybe he will listen to you. Would you let me know if I'll be alright?

At that moment I felt very selfish and realized my request was ludicrous, but then I felt Jim squeeze my hand. Had he heard me?

Neil enters the room. "Linda, it is time to leave. We need to get on the road for our trip to NYC. We'll call the hospital tomorrow to see how Jim is doing. Let's go."

Saying goodbye is difficult, for I know in my heart I won't see Jim again. Memories flood my mind. The fedora, the Brooks Brothers suits, his pointing finger, the words of wisdom, but most of all the stories from the past. He was quite a unique character and someone I am proud to know. He enriched my life.

Day 128:

The ringing won't cease, but the alarm clock isn't chiming. The room is unfamiliar. Our cell phone continues to blast its annoying chime, bringing us out of our deep slumber. While rubbing his eyes, Neil stumbles as he searches for the phone.

"Hello," he answers as I glance towards the clock. It's six a.m. I watch him listen and observe the angst upon his face. "Yes, I understand. We knew this was coming. I appreciate your calling. We're in New York City right now, but I'll call to make the necessary arrangements. We'll be back in two days. Thank you for all you have done. I only wish we could have been there with him. Goodbye."

He lays his head back down upon the pillow and tells me to go back to sleep. Jim has just passed away. There are no tears or words between us, just our own private memories.

We touch; wrap our arms around each other and fall back to sleep. Upon awakening, I hold Neil close. Too much suffering has been endured. I need the comfort and warmth of this man I have lain next to for twenty-seven years. My heart steadies to a rhythmic beat. Everything is going to be alright. I'm ready to face Dr. Gruber with whatever news he has to tell me.

Day 129:

Today is the day. Neil brings me a cup of coffee as I shower and dress. This unfamiliar room, like so many of the rooms I have stayed in, is easy to leave. I'm tired. Packing suitcases and traveling is wearing on me. I just want an end to all of this.

I'm here again, sitting in the waiting room, hoping to hear my name called soon. The magazines sitting on the table are of no interest to me. The room is crowded with waiting people. I begin to fidget. My toes wiggle, my hands twitch and I can't sit still.

As I stand up, I hear my name announced and enter the room that will determine my next move. I have been here before, but can't quite remember it until I see the doctor sitting in his chair. He is the same as I remember. Quiet and stern, with an air of confidence.

The x-rays weigh heavily in Neil's hands. He gives them to the doctor as I slump in the chair. Memories of my last visit inundate my mind. Have all of my prayers gone unanswered? Was I foolish to think I would get a reprieve? I sink lower in my seat. One single pervasive thought comes to mind. Run! I can run and escape if I really want to. I don't have to hear what is coming. My legs feel like they are bolted to the floor. I can't seem to move. There is no escape.

The pictures of my brain are set up to the light and I listen as the doctor speaks. What did he say? I'm done! No more chemo! This is impossible. I must be dreaming. I jump out of the chair, lunge across his desk and profess my love for him. He is dumbfounded, pushes me away, and tells me to get a hold of myself. I can't! He continues to stare at me like I am some sort of lunatic. My happiness soars! I don't care what he thinks of me. Nothing can ruin this moment.

"Oh my God, I have been praying for weeks and now you have answered my prayers. You have no idea what this means to me. I can only hope that you will never have to be sitting in the chair I am in right now. Because if you were you would understand how I feel at this moment."

And as I continued to sit in my seat, I composed myself and silently said a prayer to Jim. "Thank you" is all I can utter. My chemo is over two months earlier than expected. I am truly blessed.

Neil is speechless. He knows how much I have longed for this moment and is stunned at the incredible good news. But then the shoe drops. The doctor isn't quite finished talking. My elbows rest upon his desk with a grin upon my face as wide as the Chesire Cat's. He can say whatever he wants. I'm done with chemo and the results look good.

"I realize you are happy about the end of chemo, but instead of two weeks of radiation, you'll have to endure seven weeks. We've had many clinical trials with this type of tumor and find radiation is necessary. You've responded well to the chemo, so we're ending that. But to be completely sure we have eradicated the bad cells, radiation will be the final step. It's important that you follow this protocol."

Neil asks questions. I just sit, grinning from ear to ear, thinking about the poison no longer entering my body. I'll think about radiation later. For now, this one single moment, I will revel in the joy I'm experiencing. I want to dance in the street and shout to everyone that I have just been given the best present in my life. Tomorrow is another day, and there is enough time to think about radiation. Hopefully, Neil hears everything the doctor is saying.

Skipping out of the office, jumping up and down while clapping my hands, I turn to Neil and ask him, "What about this radiation thing? A piece of cake, right?"

"Not really," he replies.

You'll probably lose your hair, and there could be some serious side effects. But we won't know until we set up your appointment at home with a radiation oncologist. Meanwhile, let's just enjoy this day. When we get home, we need to bury Jim."

Day 130:

We're home. Blood work is still necessary. For the first

time in months, I enter the clinic with a feeling of elation. Everyone has heard the news and congratulations are showered upon me. As happy as I am, my compassion for the friends still battling this disease overwhelms me. My joy subsides. It's hard to feel good as I watch the people I have grown fond of still suffer. Yet their joy for me is genuine and I humbly accept their best wishes. Sorrow is in my heart. Why am I so lucky, when other people continue to suffer? There is no answer.

Day 131:

Jim's funeral is today. The feeling of sadness is omnipresent. The service is well attended and Neil delivers a eulogy that moves everyone to tears. I walk down the steps and welcome the presence of my good friends. We reminisce, as so often people do at funerals. Jim will be missed.

Day 132:

This morning brings us sunshine, but the temperature is bitter cold. It's the month of March; the beginning of spring in most places; but we are reminded that winter still holds its icy grip on us. Snowflakes dance as they swirl through the air just enough to jog our memories that winter is reluctant to go. I think about my upcoming radiation and am filled with dread. The warmth and comfort of my home eases my fear. I will muster up the courage for the next battle.

RADIATION DAZE

It has been a few weeks since my reprieve from chemo. The powerful elation I felt has come and gone. For at least a week I walked on air, tap dancing down the street, drinking in the fact that no more poison would enter my body.

But all of that has changed. It's amazing how fleeting those feelings were, and now reality has dug its claws into me. For the past two weeks, we have been driving to the radiation clinic for all of the protocol.

There were numerous blood tests, a brain mapping, a fitting for a brain mask, but most of all, I had to deal with the fear of having my brain nuked.

My first day led me to an unpleasant encounter with the receptionist. Entering the clinic alone, I signed in. Taking a seat, the lady at the desk soon called my name. She told me I needed to speak with Kathy about my health insurance. Entering the cubicle where Kathy sat, I stood and listened to her chastise me about the referral she claimed I didn't have from my insurance. My body tensed as she rambled on about my lack of understanding the process of having this paid for. I was horrified and embarrassed. I apologized for not having a referral when in actuality I was sure I had gotten one. I just stood there, while my anger and disdain for this woman grew.

We're cancer patients, not lepers. We just want to do what it takes to make us better. We don't need to hear about referrals from doctors or how we mistakenly forgot to have our health insurance send one—although in actuality mine had. As I stood at her desk, she told me we could not proceed with my brain mapping. I was flabbergasted.

"Could you explain this to me?" I asked.

"We don't have a referral from your insurance provider. In order for us to continue, you must go home and call your health insurance."

"But I'm here right now and have driven fifty miles to have this done. They told me it was all set. Are you telling me I will have to come back?"

"Well not exactly. You can go in there, but you must make sure your referral comes through. Otherwise we'll have to charge you for this procedure. As soon as you get home, call them."

I was perplexed. Was it me or was it the system? I knew she had the referral and I now felt intimidated by some office clerk on a power play. Where was the compassion? I found none in her voice. Turning my head away from her, I noticed the throngs of people in the brightly lit waiting room. Embarrassment washed over me and tears overflowed my eyes. I hurried to the restroom; the door slammed shut behind me. As I stood in front of the mirror, I watched the tears spill down my cheeks.

My name was being called. Dousing my face with cold

water while wiping away tears of frustration, I made my way to the radiation waiting room. They were ready for me. As I entered the dungeon of mega rads, the receptionist ran in.

"Mrs. McGovern. I found your referral. You're all set to go."

And she left. She'd had it all along. No apology, no good luck wishes, just a matter-of-fact statement. Her empathy for people who are sick was truly lacking as she marched out of the room with an air of self-importance. I wanted to scream at her, but I managed to restrain myself. It was important I remain calm.

The technicians led me into a heavily leaded room. Neil and I had been told what to expect, but no one really knows until it happens. And today Neil wasn't with me. I was alone.

A cold hard bed was placed in the middle of this uninviting room. The technician told me to lie down. I watched as he began to create the mask needed for the radiation. A huge alien looking machine hung above my head. The stark realization that my brain was going to be nuked, sent shivers down my spine. But today was just a simulation and brain mapping. The muscles in my body began to relax.

The technician stood by my side and asked if I was claustrophobic. I never thought I was, but subsequent MRI's have made me realize that I am. Have you ever had an MRI? If not I hope you will never have to have the opportunity to experience being in a machine that can make your heart palpitate and feel like you want to scream. A sort of panic can set in when you realize you must be inside this closed space for forty five minutes. If you have only had one, it is usually bearable, but after having numerous encounters with this test, I am not immune to the panic it causes me. I hate them. So I answered this handsome technician standing by my side, who was waiting for my reply. "Yes I am claustrophobic, but why does it matter today?" "Because we are going to put a cloth mesh over your face and you might feel like you can't breathe. Please let us know if you are okay with this procedure." he replied. "Oh, that won't bother me as long as you don't put me in that suffocating tube they call an MRI." I said.

My eyes closed tightly as he placed the mesh upon my face, which formed a mask. Breathing wasn't a problem, and soon the mask hardened as it sculpted my facial features. He bolted the mask to the table. The simulation began. Without using actual radiation rays, he was able to pinpoint the three locations on my skull that needed to be zapped with radiation. The mask was marked with three crosses, which eliminated the need for being tattooed, like so many women with breast cancer would have. I was grateful for that.

After twenty minutes of lying perfectly still, he removed the mask and told me we were done. Next week would be the real thing. I stood and walked out of the dark, leadened room that contained the bed that only sick or dying people lie on.

The next seven weeks were tough. Every morning the ritual of putting Kevin on the bus and hurrying down to Amsterdam, a fifty mile drive, was draining on us. Five days a week I received three zaps to my head. In the beginning it was easy. Nothing to it. But, just like chemo, the more you get, the worse it becomes.

I kept a journal during my passage through radiation. Later on, I wondered if I wanted to subject my readers to the tedious ritual of radiation. My answer was no. There isn't a person out there who would want to be subjected to the monotonous recollections of something they wouldn't understand. But for me, the journal became a device to help me remember what it took to survive.

For you the reader, these day-to-day recollections would be wearisome. But there were certain incidents worth telling. Many people have undergone the process of radiation, but the majority of people have never had their brain infiltrated with the rays we know in our hearts are harmful. The side effects to the brain are completely different from other treatments.

Without minimizing other people's experiences, I just want to relay to you, the reader, what brain radiation was like for me. Although cancer is frightening, having a brain tumor seemed worse. Death appeared to be imminent. After personally sharing stories with friends who had to undergo some awful treatments, my empathy was obvious, but the voyage I was taking was so unlike theirs. Remember—the brain controls everything and entering that heavily leadened room frightened me beyond belief!

WHAT A DIFFERENCE A HAIR MAKES

It had been only two weeks since the first day I entered that dreaded clinic. Everyone was so nice and yet I found myself not appreciating their kindness. Each time I arrived, I endured the mask and three zaps of radiation to my head. I had been warned about what was to happen, but put it out of my mind.

The fatigue overwhelmed me. The down comforter on our bed was light and cozy, as I snuggled myself within its warmth. Through the monitor we kept in our bedroom, I heard the echoing sounds of Kevin and Neil's laughter. My eyes were heavy from sleep, almost as if I had been drugged. I rose out of bed, shivering as the cool air hit my body. It was time to shower, get dressed and drive down for my treatment. As I turned to look at the clock, the clumps of hair on my pillow startled me. "Where did those come from?" I thought. They couldn't have come from me, even though Neil is bald. I hesitated, but mustered up the courage to run my fingers through my hair—it was still there. What was happening? While I looked in the mirror, the words from the radiation technician rang in my ears.

"You'll probably lose your hair with this radiation. If I were you, I would shave my head. There's also a good chance your hair will not grow back. Radiation tends to burn the hair follicles. Start looking for a wig."

At the time I didn't believe him. I never lost my hair during chem., so why would I lose it now. I gathered my thoughts, glanced back to my pillow and told myself this was nothing to be alarmed about. The reflection in the mirror belied what lay clumped upon the pillow. Relief washed over me. I listened to Neil playing with Kevin as I stepped into the shower. The pulse of water upon my body helped to make me feel alive. I refused to think about my treatment.

With soapy eyes I reached for the shampoo. A generous amount of the sweet-smelling cleanser lathered my scalp. Rubbing vigorously, clumps of hair became entwined between my fingers. I screamed! The sound emanating from my mouth was unlike anything I'd heard before and echoed through our home. Neil ran to my side. I sat on the cold bathroom floor with tears streaming down my face and locks of hair clenched in my fists. His arms reached out to me, but I pushed him away. There was no comfort to be found. My hair was falling out and I was horrified. It wasn't the thought of being bald that scared me, as much as the fact I was allowing them to do this to me.

Neil helped me get up off the floor. "Don't worry, Linda. It's not that noticeable yet."

But I knew it would be soon. My mind was made up. I would shave my head just like the technician advised. I dressed and got ready to go. After receiving the radiation, Neil drove me home and I slept.

The next day I called my son Eric. "Honey can you come over with your razor and shave my head? My hair is falling out in clumps and I need to face the fact that I will be bald soon."

"Sure." He replied. I waited and in a few minutes I heard the knock on the door.

Eric stood in the doorway with razor in hand and his own bald head.

"What have you done?" I asked.

"Mom, if you're going to be bald, then so am I."

My laughter rang out loud as the razor buzzed along my scalp. When he was done, we both hugged. Baldness didn't become me, but I wasn't afraid anymore. It was just hair. Turbans and wigs would have to suffice. Hopefully the hair will grow back, but if not, so be it. I just wanted to survive. Eric understood that.

And so the days droned on. Turbans were much more comfortable than the wig, so they became my fashion. I stared at my reflection in the mirror and thought about the Pillsbury Doughboy. Steroids managed to do that. My face was puffed up and my body developed a roundness I had never experienced before.

I hated the steroids. My personality changed and I had an insatiable appetite. I craved Double Stuff Oreos. If Neil wasn't able to buy them in our local grocery store I would become enraged. And the pounds packed on. I begged the doctor to take me off them, but he said he wouldn't. The steroids minimized my brain swelling from the radiation, and without them I would be very sick. So the pills were popped into my mouth twice a day.

Seven weeks of driving to the clinic weighed heavy on me. The more we went, the more tired I became. My brain didn't like radiation. The urge to sleep was so overpowering I had no choice but to give in.

One day we left the clinic and Neil asked me if I would mind driving with him to a destination about an hour away. He needed to meet with someone about a new business he was starting. As he was asking me, my eyes closed and my mind drifted off into the land of dreams. The abrupt end of the soothing, rhythmic motion jolted me awake. I was disoriented and unable to fully focus on my whereabouts. Neil was patient and waited for me to acknowledge where I was. Alongside a building was the Mohawk River. The sun was shining, reflecting its rays off the water. He gently took my hand and led me inside the building to have lunch with the woman he was meeting. My thoughts were discombobulated. I didn't speak. I struggled to finish my lunch, then finally excused myself after apologizing for my lack of social graces, and entered our car. Sleep descended upon me once more.

There is no other way to describe what was happening to me. Some days were good, but most were bad. No real pain, yet in spite of that, I felt someone had stolen important moments in my life. Most days were heavily laden with sleep. I couldn't think straight, concentrate or care about anything. The days on the calendar were marked off, helping me to understand there was an end in sight. And then it arrived. My last treatment was on the horizon.

The daffodils peeked up from the ground as we stepped into the clinic. Spring was showing signs of new life and the feeling of rebirth was upon me. This would be the final walk down the corridors of the place I had learned to hate. As I entered the place that filled me with disdain, and received my last treatment, I saw my doctor and all the people who had helped me through my seven week journey. They came out of the room which had sent deathly rays to my head and hugged me. My favorite nurse held a paper in the palm of her hand and I sheepishly took it. The paper said congratulations on completing your protocol of radiation. As I looked at this simple piece of paper, with my bald head wrapped in a turban, tears filled my eyes. All of their signatures, along with all of their best wishes were written on this so called diploma. As long as I live, I will never forget the people who gave me the strength to endure this regimen.

EPILOGUE

What can I say? I'm still here. It is four years since all of this occurred, and there is still no sign of a recurrence. My hair has grown back and the wig and turbans I bought sit in my closet. There is always the chance I might need them again. I continue to have MRI's and see my doctor every three months, but so far everything is normal. At least that is what they say.

But I'm different. My whole world was turned upside down. Does one ever recover from something so traumatic? As I sit and contemplate what could have happened, I realize I'm one of the few lucky ones. Many people with cancer don't survive, and most suffer immensely. My parents were a perfect example. But I'm not here to remind you of the many tragedies that occur every day. For once I feel I can relay a story filled with pain, suffering, and fear, but suffused with hope.

Four years later I'm still walking around feeling high on life. Our first grandson was born five months ago, so my wish has been fulfilled. No matter what happens now is of no consequence.

I realize with an ounce of sadness that none of us lives

forever. I wish we all could remain on earth for all eternity, but the day will come when we'll pass on to a better world. I have received a gift. Time! I have more of it and appreciate every minute I have been given. I wish for you, the reader, to realize every moment is precious, and to waste just one minute of your day is a crime. You must stop thinking about the past and the future. Revel in the moment. Once it's gone, there is no way to retrieve it. I learned this the hard way during the Winter of My Repose.